VOLKSWAGEN
TYPE 4

411 & 412

THE FINAL REAR-ENGINED VW CARS

Also from Veloce Publishing –

1½-litre GP Racing 1961-1965 (Whitelock)
AC Two-litre Saloons & Buckland Sportscars (Archibald)
Alfa Romeo 155/156/147 Competition Touring Cars (Collins)
Alfa Romeo Giulia Coupé GT & GTA (Tipler)
Alfa Romeo Montreal – The dream car that came true (Taylor)
Alfa Romeo Montreal – The Essential Companion (Classic Reprint of 500 copies) (Taylor)
Alfa Tipo 33 (McDonough & Collins)
Alpine & Renault – The Development of the Revolutionary Turbo F1 Car 1968 to 1979 (Smith)
Alpine & Renault – The Sports Prototypes 1963 to 1969 (Smith)
Alpine & Renault – The Sports Prototypes 1973 to 1978 (Smith)
An Austin Anthology (Stringer)
An Austin Anthology II (Stringer)
An English Car Designer Abroad (Birtwhistle)
Anatomy of the Classic Mini (Huthert & Ely)
Anatomy of the Works Minis (Moylan)
Armstrong-Siddeley (Smith)
Bahamas Speed Weeks, The (O'Neil)
Bentley Continental, Corniche and Azure (Bennett)
Bentley MkVI, Rolls-Royce Silver Wraith, Dawn & Cloud/Bentley R & S-Series (Nutland)
Bluebird CN7 (Stevens)
BMC Competitions Department Secrets (Turner, Chambers & Browning)
BMW 5-Series (Cranswick)
BMW Z-Cars (Taylor)
BMW Classic 5 Series 1972 to 2003 (Cranswick)
British at Indianapolis, The (Wagstaff)
British Cars, The Complete Catalogue of, 1895-1975 (Culshaw & Horrobin)
BRM – A Mechanic's Tale (Salmon)
BRM V16 (Ludvigsen)
Bugatti – The 8-cylinder Touring Cars 1920-34 (Price & Arbey)
Bugatti Type 40 (Price)
Bugatti 46/50 Updated Edition (Price & Arbey)
Bugatti T44 & T49 (Price & Arbey)
Bugatti 57 2nd Edition (Price)
Bugatti Type 57 Grand Prix – A Celebration (Tomlinson)
Caravan, Improve & Modify Your (Porter)
Caravans, The Illustrated History 1919-1959 (Jenkinson)
Caravans, The Illustrated History From 1960 (Jenkinson)
Carrera Panamericana, La (Tipler)
Car-tastrophes – 80 automotive atrocities from the past 20 years (Honest John, Fowler)
Chevrolet Corvette (Starkey)
Chrysler 300 – America's Most Powerful Car 2nd Edition (Ackerson)
Chrysler PT Cruiser (Ackerson)
Citroën DS (Bobbitt)
Classic British Car Electrical Systems (Astley)
Classic Engines, Modern Fuel: The Problems, the Solutions (Ireland)
Cobra – The Real Thing! (Legate)
Cobra, The last Shelby – My times with Carroll Shelby (Theodore)
Competition Car Aerodynamics 3rd Edition (McBeath)
Competition Car Composites A Practical Handbook (Revised 2nd Edition) (McBeath)
Concept Cars, How to illustrate and design – New 2nd Edition (Dewey)
Cortina – Ford's Bestseller (Robson)
Cosworth – The Search for Power (6th edition) (Robson)
Coventry Climax Racing Engines (Hammill)
Cranswick on Porsche (Cranswick)
Daily Mirror 1970 World Cup Rally 40, The (Robson)
Daimler SP250 New Edition (Long)
Datsun Fairlady Roadster to 280ZX – The Z-Car Story (Long)
Dino – The V6 Ferrari (Long)
Dodge Challenger & Plymouth Barracuda (Grist)
Dodge Charger – Enduring Thunder (Ackerson)
Dodge Dynamite! (Grist)
Dodge Viper (Zatz)
Drive on the Wild Side, A – 20 Extreme Driving Adventures From Around the World (Weaver)
Driven – An Elegy to Cars, Roads & Motorsport (Aston)
Dune Buggy, Building A – The Essential Manual (Shakespeare)
Dune Buggy Files (Hale)
Dune Buggy Handbook (Hale)
East German Motor Vehicles in Pictures (Suhr/Weinreich)
Fast Ladies – Female Racing Drivers 1888 to 1970 (Bouzanquet)
Fate of the Sleeping Beauties, The (op de Weegh/Hottendorff/op de Weegh)
Ferrari 288 GTO, The Book of the (Sackey)
Ferrari 333 SP (O'Neil)
Fiat & Abarth 124 Spider & Coupé (Tipler)
Fiat & Abarth 500 & 600 – 2nd Edition (Bobbitt)
Fiat in Motorsport
Fiats, Great Small (Ward)
Ford Cleveland 335-Series V8 engine 1970 to 1982 – The Essential Source Book (Hammill)
Ford F100/F150 Pick-up 1948-1996 (Ackerson)
Ford F150 Pick-up 1997-2005 (Ackerson)
Ford Focus WRC (Robson)
Ford GT – Then, and Now (Streather)
Ford GT40 (Legate)
Ford Midsize Muscle – Fairlane, Torino & Ranchero (Cranswick)
Ford Model Y (Roberts)
Ford Mustang II & Pinto 1970 to 80 (Cranswick)
Ford Small Block V8 Racing Engines 1962-1970 – The Essential Source Book (Hammill)
Ford Thunderbird From 1954, The Book of the (Long)
Ford versus Ferrari – The battle for supremacy at Le Mans 1966 (Starkey)
Formula 1 - The Knowledge 2nd Edition (Hayhoe)
Formula 1 All The Races - The First 1000 (Smith)
Formula One – The Real Score? (Harvey)
Formula 5000 Motor Racing, Back then ... and back now (Lawson)
The Good, the Mad and the Ugly ... not to mention Jeremy Clarkson (Dron)
Grand Prix Ferrari – The Years of Enzo Ferrari's Power, 1948-1980 (Pritchard)
Grand Prix Ford – DFV-powered Formula 1 Cars (Robson)
Great British Rally, The (Robson)
GT – The World's Best GT Cars 1953-73 (Dawson)
Hillclimbing & Sprinting – The Essential Manual (Short & Wilkinson)
Honda NSX (Long)
Honda S2000, The Book of The (Long)
Immortal Austin Seven (Morgan)
India - The Shimmering Dream (Reisch/Falls (translator))
Inside the Rolls-Royce & Bentley Styling Department – 1971 to 2001 (Hull)
Intermeccanica – The Story of the Prancing Bull (McCredie & Reisner)
Italian Cafe Racers (Cloesen)
Italian Custom Motorcycles (Cloesen)
Jaguar - All the Cars (4th Edition) (Thorley)
Jaguar from the shop floor (Martin)
Jaguar E-type Factory and Private Competition Cars (Griffiths)
Jaguar, The Rise of (Price)
Jaguar XJ 220 – The Inside Story (Moreton)
Jaguar XJ-S, The Book of the (Long)
Japanese Custom Motorcycles – The Nippon Chop – Chopper, Cruiser, Bobber, Trikes and Quads (Cloesen)
Jeep CJ (Ackerson)
Jeep Wrangler (Ackerson)
The Jowett Jupiter – The car that leaped to fame (Nankivell)
Karmann-Ghia Coupé & Convertible (Bobbitt)
Kris Meeke – Intercontinental Rally Challenge Champion (McBride)
KTM X-Bow (Pathmanathan)
Lamborghini Miura Bible, The (Sackey)
Lamborghini Murciélago, The book of the (Pathmanathan)
Lamborghini Urraco, The Book of the (Landsem)
Lancia 037 (Collins)
Lancia Delta HF Integrale (Blaettel & Wagner)
Lancia Delta Integrale (Collins)
Land Rover Design - 70 years of success (Hull)
Land Rover Emergency Vehicles (Taylor)
Land Rover Series III Reborn (Porter)
Land Rover, The Half-ton Military (Cook)
Land Rovers in British Military Service – coil sprung models 1970 to 2007 (Taylor)
Le Mans Panoramic (Ireland)
Lexus Story, The (Long)
Lola – The Illustrated History (1957-1977) (Starkey)
Lola – All the Sports Racing & Single-seater Racing Cars 1978-1997 (Starkey)
Lola T70 – The Racing History & Individual Chassis Record – 4th Edition (Starkey)
Lotus 18 Colin Chapman's U-turn (Whitelock)
Lotus 49 (Oliver)
Lotus Elan and +2 Source Book (Vale)
Making a Morgan (Hensing)
Maserati 250F In Focus (Pritchard)
Mazda MX-5/Miata 1.6 Enthusiast's Workshop Manual (Grainger & Shoemark)
Mazda MX-5/Miata 1.8 Enthusiast's Workshop Manual (Grainger & Shoemark)
Mazda MX-5 Miata, The book of the – The 'Mk1' NA-series 1988 to 1997 (Long)
Mazda MX-5 Miata, The book of the – The 'Mk2' NB-series 1997 to 2004 (Long)
Mazda MX-5 Miata Roadster (Long)
Mazda Rotary-engined Cars (Cranswick)
Maximum Mini (Booij)
Meet the English (Bowie)
Mercedes-Benz SL – R230 series 2001 to 2011 (Long)
Mercedes-Benz SL – W113-series 1963-1971 (Long)
Mercedes-Benz SL & SLC – 107-series 1971-1989 (Long)
Mercedes-Benz SLK – R170 series 1996-2004 (Long)
Mercedes-Benz SLK – R171 series 2004-2011 (Long)
Mercedes-Benz W123-series – All models 1976 to 1986 (Long)
Mercedes G-Wagen (Long)
MG, Made in Abingdon (Frampton)
MGA (Price Williams)
MGB & MGB GT– Expert Guide (Auto-doc Series) (Williams)
MGB Electrical Systems Updated & Revised Edition (Astley)
MGB – The Illustrated History, Updated Fourth Edition (Wood & Burrell)
The MGC GTS Lightweights (Morys)
Micro Caravans (Jenkinson)
Micro Trucks (Mort)
Microcars at Large! (Quellin)
Mini Cooper – The Real Thing! (Tipler)
Mini Minor to Asia Minor (West)
Mitsubishi Lancer Evo, The Road Car & WRC Story (Long)
Montlhéry, The Story of the Paris Autodrome (Boddy)
MOPAR Muscle – Barracuda, Dart & Valiant 1960-1980 (Cranswick)
Morgan Maverick (Lawrence)
Morgan 3 Wheeler – back to the future!, The (Dron)
Morris Minor, 70 Years on the Road (Newell)
Moto Guzzi Sport & Le Mans Bible, The (Falloon)
Moto Guzzi Story, The – 3rd Edition (Falloon)
Motor Movies – The Posters! (Veysey)
Motor Racing – Reflections of a Lost Era (Carter)
Motor Racing – The Pursuit of Victory 1930-1962 (Carter)
Motor Racing – The Pursuit of Victory 1963-1972 (Wyatt/Sears)
Motor Racing Heroes – The Stories of 100 Greats (Newman)
Motorhomes, The Illustrated History (Jenkinson)
Motorsport In colour, 1950s (Wainwright)
N.A.R.T. – A concise history of the North American Racing Team 1957 to 1983 (O'Neil)
Nissan 300ZX & 350Z – The Z-Car Story (Long)
Nissan GT-R Supercar: Born to race (Gorodji)
Nissan – The GTP & Group C Racecars 1984-1993 (Starkey)
Northeast American Sports Car Races 1950-1959 (O'Neil)
Nothing Runs – Misadventures in the Classic, Collectable & Exotic Car Biz (Slutsky)
Patina Volkswagen, How to Build a (Walker)
Patina Volkswagens (Walker)
Pontiac Firebird – New 3rd Edition (Cranswick)
Porsche 356 (2nd Edition) (Long)
Porsche 356, The Ultimate Book of the (Long)
Porsche 908 (Födisch, Neßhöver, Roßbach, Schwarz & Roßbach)
Porsche 911 Carrera – The Last of the Evolution (Corlett)
Porsche 911R, RS & RSR, 4th Edition (Starkey)
Porsche 911 SC, Clusker
Porsche 911, The Book of the (Long)
Porsche 911 – The Definitive History 1963-1971 (Long)
Porsche 911 – The Definitive History 1971-1977 (Long)
Porsche 911 – The Definitive History 1977-1987 (Long)
Porsche 911 – The Definitive History 1987-1997 (Long)
Porsche 911 – The Definitive History 1997-2004 (Long)
Porsche 911 – The Definitive History 2004-2012 (Long)
Porsche 911, The Ultimate Book of the Air-cooled (Long)
Porsche – The Racing 914s (Smith)
Porsche 911SC 'Super Carrera' – The Essential Companion (Streather)
Porsche 914 & 914-6: The Definitive History of the Road & Competition Cars (Long)
Porsche 924 (Long)
The Porsche 924 Carreras – evolution to excellence (Smith)
Porsche 928 (Long)
Porsche 930 to 935: The Turbo Porsches (Starkey)
Porsche 944 (Long)
Porsche 964, 993 & 996 Data Plate Code Breaker (Streather)
Porsche 993 'King Of Porsche' – The Essential Companion (Streather)
Porsche 996 'Supreme Porsche' – The Essential Companion (Streather)
Porsche 997 2004-2012 'Porsche Excellence' – The Essential Companion (Streather)
Porsche Boxster – The 986 series 1996-2004 (Long)
Porsche Boxster & Cayman – The 987 series (2004-2013) (Long)
Porsche Racing Cars – 1953 to 1975 (Long)
Porsche Racing Cars – 1976 to 2005 (Long)
Porsche - Silver Steeds (Smith)
Porsche – The Rally Story (Meredith)
Porsche: Three Generations of Genius (Meredith)
Powered by Porsche (Smith)
Preston Tucker & Others (Linde)
RAC Rally Action! (Gardiner)
Racing Camaros (Holmes)
Racing Colours – Motor Racing Compositions 1908-2009 (Newman)
Racing Mustangs – An International Photographic History 1964-1986 (Holmes)
Rallye Sport Fords: The Inside Story (Moreton)
Rolls-Royce Silver Shadow/Bentley T Series Corniche & Camargue – Revised & Enlarged Edition (Bobbitt)
Rolls-Royce Silver Spirit, Silver Spur & Bentley Mulsanne 2nd Edition (Bobbitt)
Rover P4 (Bobbitt)
Runways & Racers (O'Neil)
RX-7 – Mazda's Rotary Engine Sportscar (Updated & Revised New Edition) (Long)
Sauber-Mercedes – The Group C Racecars 1985-1991 (Starkey)
Schlumpf – The intrigue behind the most beautiful car collection in the world (Op de Weegh & Op de Weegh)
Sleeping Beauties USA – abandoned classic cars & trucks (Marek)
SM – Citroën's Maserati-engined Supercar (Long & Claverol)
Speedway – Auto racing's ghost tracks (Collins & Ireland)
Sprite Caravans, The Story of (Jenkinson)
Standard Motor Company, The Book of the (Robson)
Steve Hole's Kit Car Cornucopia – Cars, Companies, Stories, Facts & Figures: the UK's kit car scene since 1949 (Hole)
Subaru Impreza: The Road Car And WRC Story (Long)
Supercar, How to Build your own (Thompson)
Tales from the Toolbox (Oliver)
Tatra – The Legacy of Hans Ledwinka, Updated & Enlarged Collector's Edition of 1500 copies (Margolius & Henry)
This Day in Automotive History (Corey)
To Boldly Go – twenty six vehicle designs that dared to be different (Hull)
Toleman Story, The (Hilton)
Toyota Celica & Supra, The Book of Toyota's Sports Coupés (Long)
Toyota MR2 Coupés & Spyders (Long)
Triumph & Standard Cars 1945 to 1984 (Warrington)
Triumph Cars – The Complete Story (new 3rd edition) (Robson)
Triumph TR6 (Kimberley)
Two Summers – The Mercedes-Benz W196R Racing Car (Ackerson)
TWR Story, The – Group A (Hughes & Scott)
TWR's Le Mans Winning Jaguars (Starkey)
Unraced (Collins)
Volkswagen Bus Book, The (Bobbitt)
Volkswagen Bus or Van to Camper, How to Convert (Porter)
Volkswagen Type 4, 411 and 412 (Cranswick)
Volkswagens of the World (Glen)
VW Beetle Cabriolet – The full story of the convertible Beetle (Bobbitt)
VW Beetle – The Car of the 20th Century (Copping)
VW Bus – 40 Years of Splitties, Bays & Wedges (Copping)
VW Bus Book, The (Bobbitt)
VW Golf: Five Generations of Fun (Copping & Cservenka)
VW – The Air-cooled Era (Copping)
VW T5 Camper Conversion Manual (Porter)
VW Campers (Copping)
Volkswagen Type 3, The book of the – Concept, Design, International Production Models & Development (Glen)
Volvo Estate, The (Hollebone)
You & Your Jaguar XK8/XKR – Buying, Enjoying, Maintaining, Modifying – New Edition (Thorley)
Which Oil? – Choosing the right oils & greases for your antique, vintage, veteran, classic or collector car (Michell)
Works MGs, The (Allison & Browning)
Works Minis, The Last (Purves & Brenchley)
Works Rally Mechanic (Moylan)

www.veloce.co.uk

First published in March 2021 by Veloce Publishing Limited, Veloce House, Parkway Farm Business Park, Middle Farm Way, Poundbury, Dorchester DT1 3AR, England. Tel 01305 260068 / Fax 01305 250479 / e-mail info@veloce.co.uk / web www.veloce.co.uk or www.velocebooks.com. ISBN: 978-1-787115-22-4 UPC: 6-36847-01522-0

Readers with ideas for automotive books, or books on other transport or related hobby subjects, are invited to write to the editorial director of Veloce Publishing at the above address. British Library Cataloguing in Publication Data – A catalogue record for this book is available from the British Library. Typesetting, design and page make-up all by Veloce Publishing Ltd on Apple Mac. Printed in India by Parksons Graphics.

VOLKSWAGEN
TYPE 4
411 & 412

THE FINAL REAR-ENGINED VW CARS

MARC CRANSWICK

VELOCE PUBLISHING
THE PUBLISHER OF FINE AUTOMOTIVE BOOKS

CONTENTS

INTRODUCTION
A COMPANY IN TRANSITION

VW TYPE 4 – THE NEW TRADITIONAL PEOPLE'S CAR

When *Autocar* magazine first tested the VW Type 4 in 1968, it described the car as, "The best Volkswagen yet."[*] When it came to handling, the article said there was little sign it was a rear-engined car. The testers also felt the Type 4 411 set a high standard in ride comfort for the vehicle class. Indeed, it was their conclusion that much thought and ingenuity had been employed, to overcome the problems associated with the usual VW rear-engined layout. In *Autocar*'s opinion, the Type 4 solved most of the VW

The Type 4 was VW's first big car, and the last new rear-engined, air-cooled passenger car design from Wolfsburg. (Courtesy Hilmar Walde & Volkswagen AG)

problems, and retained rear-engined advantages as part of the deal. However, was this enough for the Type 4, Volkswagen and the world?

If ever there was a car that needed context to be understood, it was VW's Type 4. The VW 411 was Wolfsburg's first luxury car, and an ultimate vehicle from a company that had risen, phoenix-like, from the ashes of World War II, to become the third largest automaker in the world. Volkswagen had achieved its success by making rear-engined, air-cooled, flat-four powered vehicles: the VW Type 4 was no different, just more so. Soon VW would surprise Henry Ford's Model T, with the Beetle becoming the biggest seller of all time. If you liked that Bug, were you going to love the Type 4?

In the VW air-cooled universe one could have an economy car, sports car, a luxury automobile, do open wheeler racing, or even go off road in Baja, California. After all, Dr Porsche was still favoring rear-engined, air-cooled sportscars during the VW Type 4's life. In fact, the Porsche design

consultancy was involved in the VW Type 4's genesis. Who would question Zuffenhausen's engineering brilliance? Well, rival manufacturers from around the world, and a consumer increasingly interested in style, comfort and gadgets. In this new scenario the VW 411 and 412 had a hard time convincing prospective buyers, concerning the virtues of Wolfsburg's latest design.

The VW Type 4 turned out to be a transitional car, at a time when Volkswagen itself was in flux. A rear-engined air-cooled car, but with unitary construction, and strut type front and semi-trailing arm rear suspension. A company looking to the future, but unsure if the solution should be based on traditional Porsche/VW thinking, or that utilized by contemporary European rivals? During these years the VW 411, 412 and Beetle all rolled out of Wolfsburg, and the immortal Bug beyond even this. In the long run it was Herbie's world, other cars just happened to be there. In addition, the quality of Wolfsburg's air-cooled wares was beyond question. They had an industry trumping 24/24 warranty to prove it.

Unfortunately, the Type 4 and other air-cooled VWs were long-term vehicles, in a world that was more and more short-term thinking. Perhaps all that Big Three spiel had finally hit home? Nothing older than last year's model, and features to the eyeballs! However, once the hype had died down, and the recalls issued, one would be sitting pretty in a VW Type 4.

Marc Cranswick

Our idea of a big sedan.
The VW 411.

With the VW Type 4, Wolfsburg tried to expand its product portfolio with a luxury car. It hoped air- and water-cooled ranges could co-exist. (Courtesy Volkswagen AG)

They come with extras you'd expect
to pay extra for in a big sedan.

When you sit in a 411 you'll discover
lots of nice surprises.
That's because all around you are things
we don't ask you to pay extra for.
For instance, the 3-speed fully automatic
transmission is standard equipment.
So is the thermostatically controlled auxiliary heating system that lets you set the temperature you want. And keeps it that way.
Even when the engine is not running.
So are the cloth interiors. The metallic

paint. The undercoating.
So are the radial ply tires.
So is the electric clock. The day/night
rear-view mirror. The electric rear-window
defogger. The pneumatic windshield washers.
And the glare-proof padded dash.
(By the way, the VW 411 4-Door Sedan
comes with fully reclining posture-fitted bucket
seats that adjust to 400 positions. And even
go up and down in 5 positions.)
411s also come equipped with seat belts.

The VW 412
A luxury you can afford.

FROM HITLER
TO HERBIE
1938-1968

WOLFSBURG & THE PEOPLE'S CAR

It's one thing to outline the requirements for a people's car, but it's another to actually design it. Adolf Hitler made his demands concerning what would become the VW Beetle at the Berlin Hotel Kaiserhof in the fall of 1933. The requirements were an air-cooled, streamlined family car capable of 100km/h, with fuel consumption of 7 liters per 100km. The vehicle was to be able to carry two adults and three children, and cost no more than 990RM (Reichsmarks). The car was to look like a beetle. Hitler felt one should look to nature on the subject of aerodynamics.

Hitler conveyed these requirements to the individual he considered to be Germany's leading automotive designer: Dr Ferdinand Porsche. Dr

Porsche was a fellow Austrian, but apolitical. The requirements Hitler mentioned concerning air cooling and streamlining represented then-current 1930s advanced auto thinking. Indeed, advanced streamlining theory came even earlier with Germany's airship technology. Hitler flattened the Beetle's proposed hood profile, although this was later undone by the 1971 Super Beetle. This 1302 model's hoodline echoed the thinking of Porsche's Type 32.

The air-cooled car for the world would be put into effect by the Porsche Design Bureau. Operational from the start of 1931, Porsche had offices in Kronenstrasse to serve the automotive needs of the largely Stuttgart based industry. The thinking behind the Beetle was seen elsewhere in Porsche's work, and that of others. The Porsche Type 12 was a 1932 design by Dr Fritz Neumeyer for motorcycle maker Zundapp. It had faired-in headlamps and an aerodynamically sloping rear. The Type 12 drew inspiration from the 1923 Tatra Type 11. Then came the Porsche Type 32, designed for Germany's largest motorcycle maker NSU's Baron Fritz von Falkenhayn. Adding to the Type 12's backbone chassis, all independent suspension and rear motor, was a 1.5-liter air-cooled flat-four by Josef Kales.

Dr Porsche's contemporary Hans Ledwinka, had produced a more expensive people's car, in the form of the Tatra Type 97. Ledwinka had taken the combined ideas of backbone chassis and rear air-cooled boxer motor with flywheel cooling fan to Tatra. However, Hitler's takeover of Czechoslovakia brought an end to the Type 97.

As things stood, in May 1938 a ground-breaking ceremony attended by Hitler took place at Wolfsburg with Beetle prototypes. October 6 1938 marked the formal start of Volkswagen GmbH, and the Beetle was shown at the Berlin Automobile Show in Germany in March 1939. With 16in wheels, a differential with two spur bevel gears, maximum power of 23.5bhp at three grand and 1430lb weight, it cost the target 990RM.

German citizens could purchase the 'Bug' using an interesting hire purchase scheme, whereby a savings book of 1RM stamps would see a potential car owner, eventually, on his way to a 990RM KdF-Wagen. That was the imaginative name for Porsche's Type 60. Somehow 'KdF-Wagen' or 'Strength Through Joy car' didn't have quite the same ring to it as VW Beetle, but the Nazi regime had other ideas.

The public warmed to the concept, and Germany's Labor Front received 336,668 applications. However, even though Beetles were built before and during WWII, not one savings book Bug ever made it to Fritz Q Public. The beauty of the savings book trick was that one didn't get a car until all payments had been made! In any case, the Allies quickly saw through the scheme's true purpose: it was a way for Hitler to raise funds for the pending war.

Where would the Strength Through Joy car be built? In the Strength Through Joy town, naturally. Count Werner von Schulenberg of Wolfsburg was forced to give up his land for the project. The Count wasn't the only one having trouble with the Third Reich. VW was a politically-founded, Nazi-run factory, and private German companies had trouble dealing with the Nazis.

Out of VW's 70,000 unit WWII production, approximately 48,500 were Kübelwagens – these were the Type 82 off-roaders used by German forces. Around 32,000 wartime

By 1963, VW was racing up the global sales charts. Watch out Model T! (Courtesy Syme Magazines)

Beetles (Type 51 KdF) were produced in 1940-44, along with the Type 166 Schwimmwagen amphibious vehicle. Luck was on the factory's side when it came to surviving the war. For one, the allies considered it a target of secondary importance, as far as bombing raids were concerned. For another, a dud bomb landed on KdF Stadt factory's powerhouse. If that bomb had gone off, it would have been curtains for VW.

VW & MAJOR IVAN HIRST

By February 1945 production had stopped, due to the absence of parts and raw materials. Fortunately, plant workers didn't loot or destroy factory tooling. The factory's newness also meant it didn't appear on many maps, and was often overlooked during the campaign. After WWII, VW's factory was in the British zone, and came under the control of the Royal Electrical and Mechanical Engineers as of July 1945. In August that year, British Major Ivan Hirst arrived at KdF Stadt, and

ran the factory. He did so with the help of old-Etonian Michael McEvoy, and under Colonel Charles Radclyffe.

In peacetime it was time for a name change. To get away from the Nazi legacy, Major Hirst suggested WMW (Wolfsburg Motoren Werke). However, the VW people said that while this was okay for BMW, their focus was more than engines, they made cars. So, in spite of the Nazi connection the Volkswagen name was retained. At the time not much was thought about the association. Germany was just busy trying to get back on its feet. Given the shortage of parts and raw materials, the Major had his work cut out trying to keep production going.

The name KdF Stadt certainly had to go, and Wolfsburg has been the moniker ever since – a name in keeping with the nearby 14th century castle. It would have made the dispossessed Count mighty happy. Something of a mystery was the presence of a Tatra Type 87 at the factory. This V8 luxury car was the brainchild of Hans

This 1967 Beetle-based Baja Bug was custom built by TVR Automotive (Alabama). It has a 2110cc T1 motor with Engle W-90 cam, CB Performance Panchito 044 heads, and 61cc CNC combustion chambers. For motorvation, 7.4:1 CR Mahle 94mm pistons and barrels join CB Performance 5.325in super race rods, forged 4140 chromoly 76mm crank, forged rockers and center mount Empi D series 45 carb. (Courtesy Jamie Wiseman)

Ledwinka, and featured a rear air-cooled motor and backbone chassis, like a Beetle. In spite of the car's reputation, Major Hirst found the Tatra V8 to be a wonderful machine, with safe handling. However, he could shed no light on the reason for its presence. It was simply there when he arrived at Wolfsburg. Was the Tatra V8 a staff car for a high level Nazi official, or was VW using the design for ideas? There is no conclusive proof. However, Dr Porsche did admit to occasionally having "looked over the shoulder" of his capable contemporary.

Stories have also abounded about VW being the subject of foreign automaker interest, and about the company being offered by the German government to such companies to gain much needed hard currency for Germany's postwar reconstruction. The French government was interested in moving the whole show to France, but French automakers protested.

At the end of the 1940s, the idea of moving VW to Australia was entertained by the Australian government. The idea was for a second national car to be locally made, after the General Motors Holden. However, expert consultation advised that the VW's unorthodox nature, and associated production assembly difficulties, would make it a risky proposition. During WWII, a captured Kübelwagen had been studied

From 1962, VWoA (Volkswagen of America) had a new corporate HQ in New Jersey. (Courtesy Mike)

by Humber, for the benefit of the British car industry. Humber concluded that aside from certain points of engineering interest, there was nothing special to be gleaned from Dr Porsche's work.

After WWII, Humber was once again entrusted to evaluate the Beetle. This time they were a little more complimentary. However, in relation to its Rootes Group Hillman Minx MkIII, the Bug was judged to be underpowered and noisy. Henry Ford II took a look in 1947, but the Beetle wasn't suited to Detroit's style. The Bug was the opposite of the consumer world of front-engined, water-cooled chrome sleds with their annual tailfin makeovers. This lack of conventionality would also become an issue when VW tried to move forward in the '60s with the Type 3 and 4.

In spite of all the stories about the companies that passed on VW, Major Hirst offered another version, which he revealed in an interview late in life. The Major confirmed that companies like Ford and Rootes were interested in VW's operation, but "…

neither company was ever offered the opportunity to buy Volkswagen." He added that, after the war, "The factory just wasn't up for grabs."[1] He explained that during WWII VW belonged to the Nazis, an illegal group after the conflict. When the fighting was over VW didn't belong to anyone, so it couldn't be formally offered for sale. The way VW was and the way Germany was, it was a tough sell to anyone, even Rudi Uhlenhaut. The future star of Mercedes was invited to work at VW by Major Hirst, but declined. Apart from loyalties to the Stuttgart area, Uhlenhaut just didn't think VW had a future.

The Royal Electrical and Mechanical Engineers had originally taken over Wolfsburg as a repair facility for their vehicles. The other goal was to repair existing VWs and make new ones for civilian services. Indeed, 1800 postwar Beetles had been made by the end of 1945. Even so, the factory was scheduled for dismantling under the Morgenthau plan for German deindustrialization. To show its viability, and possible benefit to the country, Wolfsburg had to make 10,000 cars in 1946. Under Major Hirst and Co it did just that … a total of 10,020. Celebrating the 10,000th car, German workers drew a 'speis plan' on a chalkboard, which showed a glass of beer, some cabbage, a pot of sauce and a cigar.

Basic commodities were things to aspire to in postwar Germany, where it was even difficult to find enough food. In 1947 VW production fell to just under 9000 units, and some German politicians suggested it would be better for the plant to be stripped. However, the German government decided against this move, feeling VW was essential to the nation's successful reconstruction. Matters slowly improved, as currency reform of the Western zone saw the Deutschmark

A split window Type 2 Microbus outside the Big Tree Theater in Tokyo. (Courtesy Hirotaka Ishizaki)

replace the Reichsmark, and soon goods started appearing in the shops; the Major said, "It was like flowers in the desert." It was the start of the speedy economic revival of West Germany, known as the 'Wirtschaftswunder.'

HEINZ NORDHOFF COMES TO TOWN

With VW up and running, Major Hirst and colleagues agreed they needed a real car industry guy to run the show, and in Heinz Nordhoff they found one. In the words of Major Hirst, "We found a chap called Heinz Nordhoff kicking his heels in Hamburg." Nordhoff was an ex-Opel man, and had run Europe's largest truck factory. He had a war honor, so couldn't be employed in the US zone, but this was no impediment in the British sector. Heinz Nordhoff was cautious, conservative and a self-styled autocrat.

It was on January 1 1948 that Nordhoff officially became VW's CEO, but on first acquaintance he didn't think much of the Beetle. However, he saw its potential, "Professor Porsche had worked something into it that made this diamond very much worth our while polishing." Heinz Nordhoff had visited America in the 1930s, and Henry Ford

had visited Germany in the 1930s. Many Germans identified American capitalist success with Henry Ford. Therefore, it's little wonder Nordhoff was moved to follow a Model T-like, one-model policy with VW.

In what some might have considered an East German Trabant-style joke, Heinz Nordhoff improved the Beetle's quality, going plusher and more upscale in the process. On July 1 1949 came the debut of the Export Beetle (Deluxe), with nicer materials and a splash of chrome. It met the classic economic development scenario, where domestic market saturation has been achieved, and then looking to exports. Under new management VW recorded over 19,000 sales in 1948, with the first official exports to America in 1949.

1949 saw VW account for 45% of German manufacturing output. The previous year, ownership of VW had moved to the new Federal Republic, and then to the State of Lower Saxony. Even with Nordhoff installed, Major Ivan Hirst stayed on for a time, to see things settled. Not everyone shared his confidence in the selection of Heinz Nordhoff. However, with VW going well, and being confident about the

Unlike the Beetle and Squareback/Fastback, VW's Type 2 Bus didn't utilize the Type 1 platform chassis. It needed more strength. (Author)

company's future, the Major left VW in 1949. VW has maintained a connection of friendship with the Royal Electrical and Mechanical Engineers, and the Major is a legend at VW.

CEO Nordhoff said he wanted to offer good value, not be swayed by the pleadings of hysterical stylists. Detroit devoted an awful lot of money to annual restyles – it was necessary when your car was a mobile billboard for your company in the most competitive

The Type 2 engine compartment was redesigned to accept the Type 4 motor for 1972. Split window Kombis/ Microbuses are highly collectible. (Author)

consumer market in the world. VW undertook modest yearly changes to make the Beetle better, not just different. For 1949 the Bug boasted a standard Solex carb, and the hole for the starting crank handle was deep sixed. The following year the antiquated cable brakes finally gave way to hydraulic equivalents. Wolfsburg even threw in ashtrays, but was that enough?

In the early days of the North American sojourn, the modest Beetle fell on deaf ears. It took three attempts to get going, and third time was a real charm. The first try was with Dutchman Ben Pon. Pon was an ex Opel dealer, and was tied to VW's first exports in 1947. Basically he had returned to Holland with five cars. Heinz Nordhoff sent him on a US mission, but response to the funny little rear-engined Bug was muted. The second attempt was via Austrian émigré Max Hoffman. Hoffman had a number of European marques on his books, such as BMW and Porsche.

Hoffman had, and would, introduce fancy European brands to America. At the time VW contracted him for assistance, he was very successful handling Porsche's launch. Max Hoffman

Type 2 buses didn't normally come in mid-engined V8 fuel-injected form with a custom A/FX drag racing frame chassis! (Author)

was a big component in Zuffenhausen getting a foothold in America. However, when it came to a regular car, a people's car, even "The People's Car," Hoffman lacked the Midas touch. The Beetle wasn't exactly Fifth Avenue fare. Hoffman's contract was terminated, and the combined efforts of Pon, Nordhoff and Hoffman, had amounted only to around 3000 US sales in three years. High time for that charm.

When you want something done properly, you have to do it yourself, and that's what VW did. VW sent 100 personnel to America to start a real US operation. Marketing bases were established on the East and West coasts. VWoA (Volkswagen of America) formally commenced on April 15 1955, with a New Jersey HQ following in 1962. Instrumental in the success of VWoA was VW's Carl Hahn. Hahn took over VWoA in 1959, and hired the agency Doyle Dane and Bernbach to promote VW's wares. They did so with what has come to be known, as a legendary off-beat "Think Small" ad campaign.

How does the snowplow driver get to work? He certainly doesn't use a Renault Dauphine! VW's thoughtful, measured approach to North America was the polar opposite of European imports like Dauphine. Instead of shade tree mechanics and warranties not worth the paper they were written on, the Beetle owner got more. Namely a nationwide network of competent, authorized VW dealers, with an ample parts supply. Then too, the Bug was so well made and reliable, chances are you didn't need much assistance in the first place. Then there was that VW warranty. In a word, you were covered.

ONE MILLION AND COUNTING ...
In 1952 Max Hoffman's organization managed to move 601 Beetles. By 1955 VW was the top imported brand in America, with 28,097 Bugs sold that year.[2] On August 6 1955, the one millionth Beetle rolled off the Wolfsburg assembly line since the end of WWII. 1949 had seen the first CKD-assembled Beetles in Ireland! Production in Brazil, Australia and Mexico started in 1953, 1957 and 1964 respectively. With a view to servicing the increasingly important American market, the German North

This is one of two surviving VW Type 3 convertible prototypes, formerly from the Karmann Vehicle Collection. (Courtesy Volkswagen AG)

Sea port facility of Emden was opened in 1964.

The Bug was catching globally, but there was no Beetle production in America, even though America often sold more Beetles than Germany. There had been a plan to build the Bug at Studebaker's vacated US factory. However, American component suppliers weren't biting when it came to a competitively priced supply of parts. They just didn't believe such a car would ever sell big. Still, with four Deutschmarks to the dollar, and West Germany a low-cost producer, an imported Beetle was a sweet deal. In addition, the Beetle avoided the saboteur behavior of a UAW line worker. Something that had, and would continue to lay domestic brands low for years to come.

VW's rise wasn't all Beetle. In 1950 came the equally important Type 2 Transporter. It opened up a whole new avenue of air-cooled wonder. The idea, as legend would have it, came from Dutch VW importer Ben Pon,

who was visiting VW and doodled a van version as another possibility for the Type 1 chassis platform. This backbone chassis wasn't strong enough, so production T2s went to sturdy two-box section mainframes, five crossmembers, with the classic Bus body welded to the chassis.

However, it was back to backbone for VW's next major vehicle launch, the 1961 Type 3 1500 notchback sedan. The Type 3 stayed faithful to that backbone chassis: in August 1931 Dr Porsche patented torsion bar suspension and rear air-cooled flat-four, but there were differences. After a decade of purely utilitarian Bugs and Buses, the new sedan was styled with some concessions to consumer taste. The Type 3's engine was the familiar flat-four, re-engineered for lower height. That height was now only 16in, thanks to a crankshaft-driven cooling fan and an oil cooler now placed on its side.

The low height motor allowed the wagon Variant to arrive in 1962. This was followed by the stylish fastback

in 1965, when a new 1600 (1584cc) motor was added to the range. Like the Beetle, the new Type 3 was a two-door model range. It represented VW's goals of evolution, and product diversification. It was also hoped that the Type 3 would supersede the Beetle. Many have judged the Type 3 as Bug Version 2.0, but this wasn't to be. The Beetle kept on evolving, improving and selling. So much so, that in 1968 model year one could order a Beetle 1500 with semi-auto gearbox, and semi-trailing arm rear suspension. The former item was marketed as a 'Stick Shift,' and both elements were in common with an automatic Porsche 911 Sportomatic.

It was onwards and upwards for the Beetle and VW. In 1965, VW purchased German automaker DKW from Daimler-Benz. This sole surviving postwar member of the once illustrious

Auto Union, yet another Dr Porsche connection, had been Mercedes owned since 1958. In the final part of its history, DKW had become known as the maker of funny little two-stroke family cars. That said, with Mercedes money and design help, something new was afoot. The new was a F102 family car: a larger, conventional design with high output 'middle pressure' OHV inline four-cylinder.

The middle pressure motor, represented the thinking of Mercedes man Ludwig Kraus. Kraus had been involved with Daimler-Benz's dominance of Formula One racing in the 1950s, the W196 era. He would also prove invaluable to VW after the DKW buyout, as lead engineer concerning VW's next generation of water-cooled front drivers. The DKW connection seemed all about the future. In the

With the familiar VW 94.5in wheelbase and Type 1 style platform, the VW Type 3 with its new body and refinements was seen as Beetle II. The Type 3 ragtop never entered series production. (Courtesy Volkswagen AG)

The 'razor edge' Type 3-based Karmann Ghia spoke to VW's policy of product diversification. However, the model was only sold in Europe. (Courtesy Chris Wright)

interests of diversification, and moving upscale, VW utilized DKW's intellectual property to revive the Audi brand. By combining the F102 body with the middle pressure motor, Volkswagen group had the higher class, front drive 1965 Audi 70. It was the start of prestigious things.

VW had come a long way from 1948, and the new white factory kitchen as it was known. That year Heinz Nordhoff was presented with the facility, and the kitchen chef informed the CEO that 2000 chickens could be cooked simultaneously. To this Nordhoff replied, "But where do we get the chickens?" In any case Nordhoff decided this facility would best serve as the first R&D home for VW and its Bug.

STORMY WEATHER AT WOLFSBURG
Apart from the 1965 purchase of DKW, that same year saw VW GmbH become VW AG, a public company. Not merely the maker of the People's Car, but the volks could now buy shares in their

wagen; it seemed like the blue chip investment of the century. The Beetle was the Bug the world loved, little wonder Walt Disney brought the humble VW to the big screen in 1968 as Herbie 'The Love Bug.' For the first time since the Ford Model T, there was a vast sea of identical looking cars on the road. They flew out of Wolfsburg and VW's other facilities in vast quantities. However, in that legion of assembly line vehicles, what if one car made had a soul, had a heart? That would be Herbie The Love Bug!

Followers of probability theory might have given the concept some thought. There were an awful lot of VWs running around America at the time, and didn't the Big Three know it! In 1968 it was a tale of 390,379 Bug sedans, 9595 ragtops and 50,756 Type 2 Microbuses. All imported, and not a vinyl roof in sight. Yes, perhaps in all of that, there did indeed lurk a Herbie. So much cuter, and less demonic than Stephen King's Christine! "Why do so many people buy Volkswagens?" asked VWoA

● Dirk Beving is slightly self-conscious about working for the Defense Department and being a member of the reserves.

He subscribes to *C/D*, *Road & Track*, *The New Republic*, *The Saturday Review*, *Sunset* and *Time*, among others.

He has never been to an automobile race. His interest in cars is primarily practical. In 1966, his sophomore year at Occidental, a liberal arts college in the Eagle Rock suburb of Los Angeles, he bought a new VW 1300. He had wanted to buy a '55 Chevy, but his father (a Presbyterian minister turned elementary schoolteacher who brought his family from Iowa to San Fernando Valley in 1953) persuaded him not to.

Since he bought the VW, Dirk has added an Empi exhaust, Koni shocks and Dunlop radials.

Both he and his wife, Kay, who is now a welfare worker (between them they make about $15,000 a year), won United Presbyterian scholarships to Occidental ("They paid for us to go to college to become atheists"). They graduated last summer with BAs in psychology, got married and moved into a 2-bedroom apartment in North Hollywood.

Dirk Beving's pragmatic view of automobiles is not uncommon among the post-Berkeley generation now involved in making a living in society. He witnessed the Haight-Ashbury debacle. He views extremism, at either end of the scale, with reserve. At 23 he stands in the middle, conscious, aware and clearly uncommitted.

This is the hard sell for Detroit, Jerry Rubin and the Establishment alike.

**Dirk Beving:
Post-Berkeley
uncommitted**

A typical late '60s Car and Driver owner with a Bug. Empi pipes, Koni shocks and radials were the usual mods made by the VW squad! (Courtesy Car and Driver)

advertising. As if they already didn't know the answer, and were going to tell it to you anyway.

It wasn't all smooth sailing for VW. Strong sales or no, industry critics were asking about a Beetle successor. The same question was directed in Britain concerning the Issigonis Mini, in France regarding the Citroën 2CV, and in Italy that Fiat 500 was cute but increasingly quaint. Fiat had that one under control, and were in fact slowly turning up the heat on Herbie. Long time followers with their rear-engined, round looking 500 car for the Italian people, now 'Fix It Again Tony' had the biggest plans for Italian world domination since Carlo Ponti sent Sophia Loren to America!

Fiat was doing it with a range of boxy, small-engined conventional cars. Sedans like the Fiat 124 and 128 went quickly for their engine sizes, and you can pack a lot of luggage and people in a box. More worryingly for VW, the front drive 127 hatchback was lurking on the horizon. It would take the Mini's transverse thinking, but do it better in a larger "Supermini" format, shame about the rust ...

In 1967 Fiat took over from VW as Europe's top selling brand. More than that, the Deutschmark was getting strong. West Germany was no longer a low-cost producer, from which Americans could catch the Bug and not get the financial flu. Predictably, out came the critics: shareholders, bankers and politicians whaled on Heinz Nordhoff. They questioned the wisdom of his 'one-model and evolve' policy.

Critics would soon have to address their concerns to Dr Kurt Lotz. Lotz was formerly managing director of Swiss electrical giant Brown, Boveri & Cie. He came to VW in 1967, and, as second in command, was groomed to take over from Heinz Nordhoff when the long serving CEO retired in 1970. However, the best laid plans can go awry, and Nordhoff passed away in April 1968. Dr Lotz became the new CEO at a difficult time in VW's history, with the biggest question being 'what next?' What new models should VW make, where should they be made, and how could any car follow the iconic Bug? Time was a luxury VW did not have, but in 1968 the new Type 4 was a luxury VW did have.

TYPE 4
DESIGN GENESIS

DESIGNING BEHIND THE SCENES
VW gave the impression for many years of being about one car – the Beetle. However, the goal of improving ye olde Bug, and increasing its permutations, was only one Wolfsburg goal. A second was to develop new utility vehicles that utilized VW's flat-four and transaxle, in the shape of the mighty Bus and the VW Thing (as the Type 181 was known in the USA).

Then there were new body styles for the T1 platform chassis, the Karmann Ghia and the Type 3. Finally, Heinz Nordhoff, and VW as a whole, wanted a rear-engined unitary construction or unibody car. This was seen as the ultimate design evolution: witness the Porsche 911.

A unibody would open four doors to a world of practicality; indeed, there were several early coachbuilt

The Type 4 might have followed the Type 3 ragtop's fate if Heinz Nordhoff had lived longer. That is, cancelled on the verge of release. (Courtesy Volkswagen AG)

VW's EA222 of 1967, led to the four-door 411. The 1969 first model year oval headlights are visible. (Courtesy Volkswagen AG)

EA142, the Type 4's last step before production, saw a proposed notchback version. Unfortunately sales and marketing felt there wouldn't be sufficient demand. (Courtesy Stiftung Auto Museum Volkswagen)

examples already demonstrating this quality. There were four-door cars from Hebmuller and Papler, not to mention late-1940s open top police Beetles. In the 1950s, even four-door Beetle taxis were made in Berlin.[3] That would certainly have extended the Beetle's

life in Mexico, given the country's eventual requirement for four-door taxis. Porsche had anticipated a big redesign of VW's main car.

Dr Porsche had been in captivity immediately after the war, due to Porsche having to work for the Nazi

regime. On his release in 1947, it was expected that VW would approach Porsche to significantly redesign the Bug, Porsche's Type 60. This request never came, but VW did greatly use the services of Zuffenhausen, Pininfarina, Karmann and Ghia before the 1970s, for design proposals and engineering starting points. Many ideas didn't go into production, and many others didn't see the light of day. Indeed, this became an eventual criticism of the Nordhoff reign.

VW's long-standing CEO had spent much on such design consultancy, with limited production follow-up. Often, the firm, or, more precisely, Heinz Nordhoff, decided to stay mainly Type 1 based. So, the Beetle was developed with a conservative eye to cost and content, with not too much of either.

It has been contended that if Nordhoff had lived longer, he would never have sanctioned the extensive and expensive redesign work to create the Type 1 1302/1303. However, such revisions were necessary, proved commercially popular, and were Type 4 411 related. Then, there was the case of the Type 3 convertible: the Karmann-built cabrio was shown at the 1961 Frankfurt Auto Show; brochures were made, prices announced and orders were taken. However, Nordhoff pulled the plug in January 1963.

TYPE 4 – PORSCHE BY DESIGN
A 1969 UK Type 4 ad stated, "It's more Volkswagen than you'd expect." The four-door quality of the new VW 411 was on show. To be precise, the easy ingress and egress afforded by four apertures. However, VW said it wouldn't hold it against you if the two-door was chosen over its new German Quattroporte because, "We know it looks more like a Porsche that way." In reality it was more than a joke – one

The public never even got to see pictures of the planned five-door Variant. It seemed the coming of Audi and NSU in VW Group was dividing resources from the air-cooled models. (Courtesy Stiftung Auto Museum Volkswagen)

Heinz Nordhoff felt the VW 311 was much more important for VW's future than the Type 4. However, by 1969 Nordhoff had passed away, and the 311 was cancelled. (Courtesy Stiftung Auto Museum Volkswagen)

could make some visual and technical connections between the 1964 Porsche 911 and the 1969 VW 411 coupe. Long before either came to fruition, Porsche had been doing commissioned design work, at VW's behest, on the subject of a two-door unibody, rear-engined, air-cooled car. Such work would certainly have been of benefit to Zuffenhausen in developing the 911, work on which started in 1959.

A formative unibody study, came in the form of the Porsche Type 402-VW Kleinwagen of the late 1940s. This design was followed up with the Porsche T534, formally commissioned by VW in March 1952. This small unibody VW Klein-Sportwagen was a two-door, four place car, with a lightweight rear, air-cooled boxer motor. Although VW never sent a formal request to do a new Beetle, it could be judged that the T534 was along such lines. After all, the iconic Bug (T60) was already 15 years old!

The Porsche T534 was tested extensively by Zuffenhausen, and was shown to Heinz Nordhoff in

October 1953. It should be noted that Dr Nordhoff had a good working relationship, and friendship, with Ferry Porsche. Unfortunately, in this instance Nordhoff gave orders to destroy the T534. It was the first time Heinz Nordhoff passed on a Beetle alternative, preferring to improve the Type 1 instead. Even so, VW commissioned Porsche to do more unibody design proposals in the 1955-59 era. Zuffenhausen's work built on the T402/534 experience, and development was in conjunction with the Budd Steel Corporation of Philadelphia. It's important not only to design a car, but to work out how to productionize it or build it too.

This continued unibody work produced the Porsche coded T672, T675 and T728. The last being an 800 to 900cc rear-engined unibody two-door, that VW adopted in 1958 and worked on until the early 1960s. So it was that Porsche T728, became VW's EA53/1 to EA53/7. EA stood for Entwicklungsauftrag, or Design Assignment. In building this design

series of prototypes, bodies were designed by Porsche, and later on by Italian styling house Ghia. Simultaneously, VW and its Brazilian subsidiary VW do Brasil, were working on new bodies for the Type 1 chassis, and the new 'Flachmotor' to go with such stylish bodies.

The cars in question were the Type 1 based Type 3, and Brazilian 1600 Variant II, both of which successfully saw high volume production. However, the EA53 series' run mostly came to an end with EA53-6. This sixth prototype suffered an accident, which led to the series being re-evaluated. Indeed, given the number of model proposals, Beetle alternatives and upscale possibilities, it seems Wolfsburg was spoilt for choice, while VW was on its way to becoming the third

largest automaker in the world. The corporation's problem was similar to that of Apple Inc in the 2000s: all those variations on the iPhone, but what would be the next big step?

EA142 ... CLOSER TO THE 411

For VW, the decision regarding EA53-7 was simple. The proposal had become too big and heavy for its original purpose, so it was ended. It's reasonable to assume that the original purpose was to replace the Bug. However, EA53 was not wasted, its ideas went into EA142, which would lead to the Type 4. Indeed, as of October 1962, EA142 was seen as an eventual Type 3 replacement. This was logical for the era. Car makers used to produce new and old model ranges side by side, for a number of years.

The prototype VW 411 convertible at 2018's Techno Classica in Essen. In this era an Audi 100 ragtop was also in the works. However, management favored Audi for glamor, and both would have been victims of pending North American safety rollover tests. (Courtesy Matti Blume)

Gijs van Lennep and Jooks Klein in their 90 horse prototype 411 coupe, on the way to 4th in class in the 1969 Monte Carlo Rally. It was behind three Porsche 911s! (Courtesy Volkswagen AG)

The 1969 model year VW 411 was Dr Kurt Lotz's Christmas present to the VW faithful ... and the world! (Courtesy Lutz Gaas)

Then too, the Type 3 was subsequently seen as a budget Type 4. The latter had a unibody, a more advanced design, and, in VW evolution, the ultimate goal.

Pininfarina produced the basic styling for EA142, but early prototypes had angular bodies designed by styling house Ghia, during those pre-Ford times. In any case, the new semi-trailing arm rear suspension was in evidence, and Pininfarina's rear styling carried through from EA142 to the production 411 largely intact. Between August 1964 and February 1968 no less than 45 EA142 prototypes were created, with six having steel sunroofs. Styling proposals and scale models in September 1966 went towards finalizing the two-door 411. In October that year the first EA142 prototype with oval headlamps was created. So, 411 styling could be regarded as set by this hour.

In coming up with the definitive 411, 1966 saw a car with 2500mm wheelbase, 4490mm length and 950kg weight. The actual production 411 wound up 35mm longer and 70kg heftier. By April 1967 various body designs were at hand. EA222 was the four-door 411, the Type 4's raison d'etre; EA237 was the two-door

version and EA239 was a two-door cabrio. EA223 and EA240 were three- and five-door Variants, respectively. Regarding EA240 no photos, or even drawings, have ever come to light. That said, the body crease lines of the production 1970 411E Variant provide a real-life what if?

The marketing department judged the five-door EA240 Variant's sales potential as too low, so it wasn't taken any further. In the sea of possibilities VW commissioned Pininfarina to do some notchback and cabrio studies, EA237 and EA239 respectively. Concerning the latter, Karmann also gave it a try later. This was understandable, given the company's involvement with the earlier aborted T3 cabrio. The Type 4 was already in production when the Karmann 411 Cabrio was made in September 1968. The cabrio was coded Model Hamburg, and was even displayed at the 1969 Frankfurt Auto Show.

SO MANY POSSIBILITIES

VW management wasn't interested in Model Hamburg. Karmann also presented to VW an alternative two-door 411. This was a three-door hatchback version of the Karmann Ghia Type 14, predictably called T143. Once again, VW management said no to this proposal, and to the April 1967 Pininfarina EA237 Type 4 Notchback. The Type 4 Notchback was a stylish machine; subjectively it used the T4's extra length to create a more handsome coupe than the 1961 T3 1500 Notchback. The T3 Notchback had been withdrawn from the Swedish market at the end of 1965. As per VW sales and marketing's EA240 decision, management may have judged a Type 4 Notchback's sales potential to have been too limited. Another possibility taken no further.

Audi was in the ascendancy in the VW Group. Management favored the two-door Audi C1 100 sedan, over

Four 1969 411s at a 2014 International 411/412 meet in Arnhem, Netherlands. (Courtesy Lutz Gaas)

1969 411s in Sassenberg, Westphalia Germany in 2015. (Courtesy Lutz Gaas)

a Type 4 Notchback. Given Audi's success in upscale segments, "Gee, it looks so much like a Mercedes!" said the middle class housewife, the decision may have been justified. The 411 Notchback (Type 22B) sits in the Wolfsburg Motor Museum. Its conventional styling, combined with the '69 MY headlamps, presents yet another T4 'what if.' So too the luxury models VW also had in the works. For one there was a 1960-66 rear-engined, flat-six-cylinder EA128 limousine and EA151 Variant being planned. More realistically, a Super Deluxe Executive version of the 411 four-door was considered.

The Super Deluxe 411 four-door was planned to have separate, contoured rear seats, like a Rover 2000 or higher level BMW sedans. Effectively this 411 would have been a four-seater, with an armrest between the two rear occupants. Practically good enough for Chancellor Adenauer, if a little after his time, but sadly,

neither the six-cylinder EA128/151, nor Super Deluxe 411 saw actual production. That said, the EA223 three-door Variant was introduced for the 411's second production year, and proved popular. Pre-production of the 1969 model year Type 4 range, 411 two and four-door editions commenced in May 1968.

VW was nothing if not busy. Close to the end of development Type 4 alternatives were designed, built and tried. Once again, and typical of VW during the Nordhoff era of the '60s and immediately thereafter, the ideas were mostly not followed up. However, one concrete example did, kind of, make it through. A high-performance 411 two-door was considered. With 90 horses, as opposed to the 411's debut 68bhp 1700, the coupe was lively and successful at the 1969 Monte Carlo Rally. Porsche stalwart Gijs van Lennep did the driving, with Jooks Klein as navigator. The pair were racing under the banner of Dutch importer,

The Type 4 was never intended to replace the Beetle. The big VW 411/412 fulfilled its commercial role as an upscale, large European family car. (Courtesy Hilmar Walde)

The VW Type 4 sold at a similar rate to the 1970s BMW 5 series. VW's new big car joined a crowded market segment. (Courtesy Hilmar Walde)

and VW historical figure, Ben Pon's Automobielhandel NV. The hi po 411 came 16th overall and 4th in class. The only cars in front were three Porsche 911s!

In the 1980s, much was made concerning the Skoda 130 Rapid Coupe being the poor man's Porsche 911. However, in light of Zuffenhausen's design input concerning the Type 4, and its technical layout, that accolade was more appropriate for the VW 411. Indeed, the fact that the Type 4 even saw the light of day was with some help from Porsche. In the competition between the many possible projects at VW, the Type 4 could have fallen through the cracks. Certainly Nordhoff's decisional paralysis, and penchant for project cancellation, wouldn't have helped. However, great were the ties between VW and Porsche engineering design camps, in those pre water-cooled days.

After all, VW had got Dr Porsche to sign an agreement that he would not design a Beetle rival for another automaker … until 1973! There were staunch traditionalists at VW that had been working with Porsche, on this goal of a rear-engined unibody car since the late '40s. They pushed for Dr Kurt Lotz, Nordhoff's successor, to make the Type 4 a production reality. With a little assistance from the West German press, the Type 4 story came sooner than planned. Magazine publication *Der Spiegel* was going to scoop VW, courtesy of a spy photo.

In the modern world, car spy photos are no big deal. However, for an all new VW in 1960s West Germany, it was monumental. The Beetle's adoption of an optional factory fitted crank handle and sliding metal sunroof was easily the country's biggest news item of 1964! So it was that VW's hand was moved, to show a publicity photo of the 411 four-door sedan on May 20 1968. The Wolfsburg PR department demanded it. On July 4 of the same year, the first official Type 4 Variant pictures were released. They concerned the three aperture version, naturally.

VW'S FIRST
BIG CAR – THE 411

Thrust into the position of CEO, VW's Dr Kurt Lotz had an unenviable task in 1968. Apart from running the world's third biggest automaker, he had to oversee the car that would 'replace' the Beetle. The Beetle was, and is, the most popular car of all time, and allowed VW to join the Global Three in the first place. However, first things first, and the new Type 4 was Lotz's baby step. It was the first all-new VW under his watch. Dr Lotz officially announced the new model, at a VW shareholder meeting.

The Type 4's role must be stated from the outset. It was Heinz Nordhoff's move to push VW upscale, with a traditional VW rear air-cooled engine layout, in a price segment previously alien to Wolfsburg. The Type 4 was never intended to replace the Type 1 (Beetle). Before his death on April 12 1968, Heinz Nordhoff clearly stated VW's position. The smaller Type 5, the planned VW 311, was more crucial to the company's future than the Type 4. In other words, replacing the Bug would fall to the Type 5, or

any other machine that could fill its immense tire tracks.

THE 411'S MANY FEATURES
The Type 4 411 was more a niche product by VW's high volume production standards. It was large, in European terms, an uber Bug for the VW devotee who liked to dream big, if you will. That dream came true at the 1968 Paris Auto Salon, where the new VW 411 made its international debut. With that launch the Type 4 made VW history, with a number of innovations for the marque. First and foremost, it was the first VW with unitary construction. Secondly, it was the first Volkswagen to offer four doors.

Unfortunately, this practical extra set of doors was limited to the Type 4 sedan, never the production Variant. However, one new item common to all Type 4s, and it even took its name from the Type 4, was the Type 4 engine. As per previous Wolfsburg flat fours, this too was an overhead valve, pushrod air-cooled unit of alloy construction. The new motor

Car dealers from the '50s through to the '70s used promotional scale models and boxes like this. It was perfect for showing the Type 4's unusual (for VW) features. A four-door layout, roomy rear and monster 'frunk!' (Courtesy Lutz Gaas)

also lived behind the transaxle line, no VW surprises there. However, the differences lay in the detail. There were many advancements, and they were necessary.

The 1930s VW flat-four, like the Beetle it went into, was a technical marvel of its time. Family cars of the day had all cast iron, side valve engines for the most part. Plus, often troublesome water cooling systems. Yes, in the past, radiators, water pumps and rubber hoses were a real liability. The so called VW 'E' motor was an oversquare, magnesium-cased boxer unit, with attached tinwork to aid heat transfer. VW wanted an engine like this for the Beetle, but it had to be durable and meet Hitler's low total Beetle 990 reichmarks price tag. The 984cc solution was created by a young 33-year-old Austrian called Franz Reimspiess. Not content with virtually reinventing the wheel for over 21 million car owners, Reimspiess also designed the VW logo, which is still in use today.

Many of those Type 1 motors are still chugging along, but there were problems. The flat fours used in T1 (Beetle/Karmann Ghia), T2 (Bus) and T3 (Notch/Square/Fastback) didn't have a conventional oil filter. They had a sump mesh around the oil pump pick up to strain out large objects. However, for the most part, owners were tied to a frequent oil change schedule of 3000 miles. A domestic car could easily double that. In addition, sump capacity was quite small, at a mere 2.5 quarts. With no filter, and a reliance on engine oil as the main medium for heat transfer, this was an area of concern. It was the reason so many VW off-roaders added an oil filter.

The T4 motor was the first VW flat-four with a factory-designed and fitted oil filter system. The latest Wolfsburg design was physically larger and more durable than the T1 engine. The T4 did have the T3's low height advantages of a crankcase driven cooling fan and horizontal oil cooler. However, it wasn't the 160lb lightweight unit found in early '50s Bugs. On the plus side, the T4's aluminum case didn't get dirty as quickly as the T1's magnesium case. As a low and wide power unit, the T4 motor would need an aftermarket adaptor kit to go into a Beetle. In addition, VW redesigned the T2 Bus' engine compartment for 1972 model year, so it could accept the T4 motor. That year, it became an optional Microbus motor in Europe, and the standard powerplant in America.

To go with the 411's many refinements, the T4 motor had an additional electric cooling fan. This helped with heating the passenger compartment. The usual VW practice saw the engine-driven cooling fan blow through a heat exchanger that derived heat from the exhaust system. With

Early on, the VW Type 4's styling had quite a few admirers. (Author)

the Type 4, the electric fan cut in at low engine rpm to blow more air when the engine-driven fan wasn't spinning too fast. The latest VW boxer motor was also more performance oriented than your average Bug motor. Most T1 engines, be they single or dual port, have one Solex carb connected to the cylinder heads via a long intake manifold. The arrangement was set up for good gas mileage.

Early 411s had two Solex 34 PDSIT carbs and a relatively high (for a VW) comp ratio of 7.8:1. Power and torque stats, using DIN net figures,

A 1969 UK Type 4 ad remarked that the 411 coupe was not unlike the Porsche 911. (Courtesy Lutz Gaas)

Der Große aus Wolfsburg.

Der neue VW 411.

were 68bhp at 4500rpm and 91lb/ft at 2800rpm. In other respects, the T4 motor was a lot like the T1 flat-four. As an upscale large European car, the 411 needed an oversquare, tractable engine with good low rpm torque, and an ability to cruise at high speed sans strain. Well, that sounds mighty like the original Beetle thinking! So, it comes as little surprise that the T4 motor's dimensions were 90x66mm. A large bore and short stroke for the EA engine's 1679cc.

So it was, that VW had a new powerplant for the European large, luxury car market. Wolfsburg could claim 0-50mph in 11.5 seconds, and a 90mph top speed for four-speed 411s. More importantly for this class of car was the Type 4 motor's smooth power delivery – as refined as the much loved small German sixes, an alternative to the Ro80's Wankel rotary, and so much nicer than the usual coarse inline family four banger. *Consumer Reports* remarked that the 1970 Audi 100 LS's

middle pressure four was somewhat 'dieselish' in refinement at low speed. Generally, it ran rough and sounded harsh.[4]

To go with the 1.7-liter boxer motor, one would expect four on the floor – par for the course, given this was a European car and a VW. In common with all Bugs from 1961, that four-speed was all synchronized, but the gearing was new. Deviating from VW orthodoxy, top gear was a direct one to one, rather than an overdrive ratio. The ratios were 3.81 (1st), 2.11 (2nd), 1.40 (3rd), and 1.00 (4th), backed by a 3.73:1 final drive ratio. First gear was shorter than the Beetle's equivalent, but the taller T4 final drive ratio meant 1st wasn't the usual VW stump puller – that jack rabbit start gear, which allowed countless Bugs to race off the line, and pull out in front, much to the chagrin of other road users.

The 411's other choice, shared with the T3, was an automatic option. Not the semi auto affair first seen on

The Type 4's special flat-four being installed at Wolfsburg. As it was wider than a T1 flat-four, the T4 motor needs an aftermarket kit to fit a Beetle. (Courtesy Volkswagen AG)

1968 Beetle 1500s, but a real, honest to goodness, three-speed torque converter automatic. The Type 4 411 was surfing a new wave in European car automation and modernity. For many years automatic transmission was rarely found on European cars, even with expensive cars. After all, that's what chauffeurs were for. Indeed, one Triumph 2000 ad said the car's optional autobox was the next best thing to having one's personal Jeeves!

Even as late as 1955, Daimler-Benz didn't have an automatic option, in spite of their many innovations, including the motor car itself. In 1956, with a need to appease American luxury car buyers, they sourced an automatic from US company Borg Warner: the American origins of the three-speed torque converter unit for the Mercedes 300c, inspired the moniker 'Detroit Gear.'[5] By the mid-60s a European buyer didn't have to reach an exalted MB 300c price point to enjoy shiftless driving. They were desiring labor-saving automatic

chokes and automatic transmission in less expensive upscale cars. Fortunately, automatic transmissions started becoming available for smaller displacement non V8 engines.

So, VW followed Mercedes, Jaguar and BMW by going to Borg Warner. Like the early 1969 411 ad said, "Designed by us, for us." To be more precise, VW's automatic transaxle was developed in conjunction with Borg Warner. It was a conventional three-speed torque converter unit, with epicyclic gearbox. The VW/BW 003 autobox was the first fully automatic gearbox offered by VW, and was available on the 1969 model year Type 3 and Type 4s. The 1968 Beetle 1500 had seen an automated 'Stick Shift' manual. However, with the 003 design VW had pulled out in front of Porsche, with an eight-year lead!

In the UK it was a £145 option, in America it was standard on Type 4 four-door sedan and Variant wagon; either way the VW owner didn't have to do anything. A solid black knob on a 7in chrome lever controlled the 003

Transaxle assembly at Wolfsburg, concerning the fuel-injected 411E/LE in 1970. When specified, the Eberspacher gasoline heater was fitted above said transaxle. (Courtesy Volkswagen AG)

box from the floor, not the column. At a time when there was some international variation in automatic shift patterns and naming practice, the shift quadrant was to the left of the shifter and stated PRN321. White script lay on a black background, with no illumination. Odd, given such lighting was essential at night and expected.

There was no repetition of the quadrant script on the dashboard, or top of the steering column facing the driver, as per contemporary cars. However, for 1971 position '3' was renamed the more conventional 'D' for drive. One could only start the engine in neutral, with stick shifting into reverse 'R' or park 'P' only possible if the shift knob was lifted.

In operation, gears were selected automatically using a brake band, rather than the very latest clutch-only method. With 003, the brake band braked one of three servo-operated multi-plate clutches. In other words, gearbox parts were braked to change gear. VW claimed superb frictional efficiency for its autobox. It said it was so free of resistance, it could be turned by hand out of the car. That is, the automatic took so little power, you could push the car in drive 'D.'

In 1969 model year the 003

automatic was an expensive $189 Type 3 option, so standard inclusion on most American Type 4s was a boon. Naturally, the percentage of automatic equipped cars in North America, import and domestic, was on the rise. This made the 411's automatic a necessity, not a luxury. Then, too, the near-luxury class Audi 100LS didn't even offer automatic transmission on its 1970 North American debut. However, the news wasn't all good: lack of fluid changes and age can lead to brake bands stretching. The automatic took 3.9 quarts of Dextron type ATF fluid. This stuff was corrosive, and no friend to the automatic's cork oil pan gasket.

Maladies aside, Volkswagen's three ratios – 2.65 (1st), 1.59 (2nd) and 1.00 (3rd) – were welcome in the late '60s era, and into the '70s, when too many cars still had two-speed automatics. Chevrolet's Powerglide, Toyota's yesteryear GM Hydra-Matic-style Toyoglide, and Honda's later Hondamatic were chosen to cut cost, save space or to solely deal with low speed stop-start city driving. Only in the lightweight C2 Corvette did it work. Many critics of the time mentioned the benefit of a three-speed automatic's intermediate 'passing' ratio, and VW Type 3 and Type 4 had it.

With a torque converter automatic, there is the 3 to 1 torque amplification of said torque converter at low speeds. This eliminates the need for one ratio, making the three-speed torque converter automatic equivalent to a four-speed manual. That is, provided the engine makes a goodly amount of torque. Hence, top gear in both gearboxes having a direct 1 to 1 ratio. A three-speed automatic was much better in performance, economy and refinement than the familiar Powerglide. Two-speed boxes have that ski slope effect of building a great

Beide Variant-Varianten bekommen Sie mit fortschrittlicher Technik.

Mit VW Automatic.

Sie kommt in beiden Wagen als ein Extra. Dafür nimmt sie Ihnen das Kuppeln und Schalten ab. Somit können Sie sich stärker konzentrieren. Auf den Verkehr.

Motor und Automatic sind gut aufeinander abgestimmt. Die Automatic schaltet schneller und präziser als Sie es können. Außerdem beschleunigt der Wagen seidenweich. Ohne zu rucken.

Mit electronischer Benzineinspritzung.

Im VW Variant 411 E kommt die elektronische Benzineinspritzung serienmäßig. Im VW Variant 1600 als ein Extra.

Ein Computer reguliert die Einspritzung. So erhält der Motor bei Leerlauf, Schubbetrieb, Vollast und allen anderen Betriebszuständen immer genau das passende Gemisch. Und Sie erhalten einen Wagen mit zusätzlichen Sicherheitsreserven. Durch bessere Beschleunigung. Und einen Motor, der extrem elastisch und wirtschaftlich ist.

Electronic fuel-injection and a modern fully automatic gearbox were offered by VW's Type 4. Here, factory literature mentions that the former was an option on the Type 3 (1600). (Courtesy Volkswagen AG)

stack of revs in low gear, very noisily, only to fall off the torque curve going into top.

The Type 4 automatic avoided the indignity of losing a lot of speed on an incline because top is too tall, and the vehicle is going too fast to engage low. More than that, the 411 automatic did it with some style. *Road & Track*'s time to pass a car going at 50mph, a 50-70mph acceleration stat, showed the 411 in a good light. The journal's time for the fuel-injected 1971 411E four-door was 7.1 seconds. A lively car for the era was the 130 horse Volvo 142E four-speed. It was a sedan as quick or quicker than the contemporary Alfa Romeo 1750 Berlina or BMW 2002. The Volvo's passing time was 7.2 seconds. The six-cylinder 3-liter, fuel-injected '72 Volvo 164E cut that time to 6 seconds flat. However, the Volvo 164E automatic was a much more expensive, larger engined car.

Comparing automatic to automatic,

Road & Track's overall gas mileage figures for the VW 411E and Volvo 164E were a respective 22.5mpg and 17.7mpg. VW's laid back Type 4 flat-four retained its 8.2:1 compression ratio, even after the North American industry wide, emissions law driven, compression ratio drop. Therefore, a 1971 VW and 1972 Volvo could be fairly compared. In addition, the 411 automatic used a slightly taller 3.67:1 final drive, versus the four-speed's 3.73 ratio. So, the 411 automatic had the overtaking flexibility, economy and refinement the upscale compact buyer was looking for.

The 50-70mph overtaking a truck on a two lane highway time is of much more practical value than standing start acceleration runs. A very rapid car of the day, the Mazda RX2 four-speed coupe managed 50-70mph in 5.5 seconds. However, with the Mazda registering 17mpg overall, the VW 411's compromises seemed good enough.[6]

In the secret agent-obsessed Swinging Sixties, VW speed specialist Empi made a swing axle compensating spring to keep your Bug sunny side up! (Courtesy Empi Inc)

BYE-BYE TORSION BARS!

The Type 4 had some VW changes one could see, and some one couldn't see. The four-door body availability was plain to see, so too the bigger interior. Previous VW cars sported a 94.5in wheelbase to go with their platform chassis. However, the new 411 sat on a bigger 98in wheelbase. The better accommodation afforded by unitary construction was very apparent after the snug Bug. No one could ever accuse the 411 of being narrow or cramped. Even more than this, the Type 4 brought a complete suspension change, that was bookended by the Type 1. In 1968 the T1 Beetle 1500 semi-automatic, had semi-trailing arm rear suspension. In addition, the 1971 1302 brought MacPherson strut front suspension to the Bug.

The 1302's layout was started in 1969 by the 411, but whereas the Super Beetle retained the familiar VW rear torsion bar suspension for spring duty, the Type 4 was all coil, front and rear. At the front, space saving MacPherson struts, a Ford legacy, lower control arms, coils, conventional dampers and front swaybar; at the rear, semi-trailing arms, coils and normal shocks. Under the skin, the 411 was late 20th century conventional, like a Porsche 911. However, Dr Porsche's beloved torsion bars were absent.

Before 1971 model year the new suspension layout was a 411 exclusive in camp VW. The reason for the major change in VW thinking was to bring safer, more neutral handling to its rear-engined air-cooled cars. The torsion bars and swing axle were rugged, the latter had fewer moving parts than a semi-trailing affair, but like the stock T1 motor the traditional VW suspension was no utopia. Dr Porsche had worked four wheel independent suspension into the 1938 Bug, but it was pretty stiff. Not unlike the also all independent suspension of the C2 or C3 Corvette.

The ruggedness and simplicity of the old VW suspension was great in the days when the average road was really average. However, by the mid-60s people were getting weary of the rear swing axle's big camber change, jacking up, and a propensity for sudden oversteer. Whether the rear

With the Type 4 sharing its suspension layout with the Porsche 911, the Fuchs wheels are a valid custom touch! (Courtesy Lutz Gaas)

compensating spring came from Empi or the factory, easier and safer road control favored rear semi-trailing arms. As was seen on the later Super Beetle, the suspension reworking brought safer handling, and improved ride comfort, although *Consumer Reports* and *Road & Track* disputed the ride benefit concerning the Super Beetle.

You certainly wanted the new front and rear suspension in one VW car. With the Nader Corvair attack fresh in the memory, VWoA eliminated swing axle rear suspension from the Beetle and Type 3 by 1969 model year. However, as *Road & Track* found when sampling a T3 Squareback automatic in December 1968, combining the old front suspension with the new rear semi-trailing arms produced an awkward result. The parallel trailing arm/torsion bar front end and semi-trailing arm/torsion bar rear, made for greater low speed understeer, and a twitchiness alien to past VWs.

It seemed better to go all 'old skool' like a Karmann Ghia, or all new like the '71 MY Super Beetle and Type 4. Whatever the suspension in a rear-engined car, keeping to the manufacturer stated tire pressures was crucial to maximize safe driver control. Another control aid was the radial tire, which the Type 4 was equipped with; they were an established European item, but a newcomer on the American scene. If the suspension was tuned to the properties of the radial tire, the benefits were higher cornering speeds, improved ride comfort, and better tire life, compared to bias belted equivalents.

The 411's tires were 155-15 radials on a 15x4.5in steel rim. However, many VW enthusiasts fitted wider aftermarket aluminum rims, from VW speed specialist Empi. The Type 4's weight distribution was a very normal,

by VW standards, 45/55% front to rear. It promised safer handling on the limit. The steering system was via recirculating ball, like a Mercedes or BMW. This type of steering was a little vague about the straight ahead, but was very good for absorbing road shock. This made it an expected system on an upscale European sedan. Power assistance was unavailable, but given the traditional VW rear weight bias, it was unnecessary.

Steering wheel turns lock-to-lock wasn't slow at 3.5 turns, but it wasn't the Super Beetle's near Corvette-like 2.7 turns. Similarly, the 411's 37.5ft turning circle, while not jumbo sized, wasn't the 1302's handy 31.5ft. The reason the Type 4 wouldn't be called on to serve as a London taxi any time soon was VW engineering's desire to work in a decent sized frunk. At 400 liters (8.1ft^3), the main front luggage compartment was large, flat and useable. Unlike a domestic car trunk with inhibiting live axle, one didn't

The 1969 Type 4 411 undergoing type approval crash testing. This entailed a head-on run into a barrier at 50km/h (31mph), with a set legal limit on steering column intrusion. (Courtesy Volkswagen AG)

The optional Eberspacher preset timer allowed interior heating to be arranged in advance. The two-turn signal indicator lamps show this 412 Variant binnacle to be a 1973 unit. (Courtesy Ron Wolff)

arrive at the trunk measurement using golf balls. There was a further 2.1ft³ stowage well, behind the rear seat. However, it was shallower than the equivalent well in the Type 1. Like the Bug, it was also only accessible from inside the car. Still, unlike many hatchbacks, at least the luggage compartment was concealed.

A SAFER VW
At the time the Type 4 was launched, environmental and passive auto safety concerns were looming large. This was especially so concerning VW's major market, the good ol' USA. Here, lobby groups were successfully influencing senators to bring legislative change. The coming 1970 Muskie Smog Bill, that would eventually bring the apocalypse in North American car performance, that was 1975. On the positive side, dual circuit braking

systems and collapsible steering columns, along with safety dashboards and switches, were to the good.

VW had kept up to speed with auto safety. Apart from having a stout body structure, the Beetle had easy to use three-point inertia reel front seatbelts, head restraints, and a collapsible steering column, before such items became federally mandated. More than that, Cornell Aeronautical Laboratory Inc had carried out a fuel system integrity test. This involved crashing a Bug into a barrier at 41.8mph. Although the filler cap and fuel line connection were knocked loose, and the gas tank distorted, there was no split or puncture.

In September 1971, just a few months after the 411's North American debut, Ralph Nader and his Center for Auto Safety released a report entitled "The Volkswagen: An Assessment of Distinctive Hazards." This report called into question the safety of the Beetle and Bus. Although high in emotion and public impact, the study was criticized by the automotive media for two reasons. Firstly, Nader & Co cherry-picked facts and data, to launch their next attack on the motor car, post Corvair. Secondly, the VW Beetle and Bus were unique in the North American market. There weren't any high volume selling small cars or buses of the VW's ilk. This made statistical comparisons, with like-sized vehicles, impossible.

Cornell's data also showed the median age of the VW driver to be 25, ten years younger than the North American average. Insurance company data always shows young drivers and drivers of two-door cars, tend to have more, and more severe, accidents than other demographic profiles. Such owner nature realities may partly explain why older, pre Super Beetle Bugs have greater risk and degree of

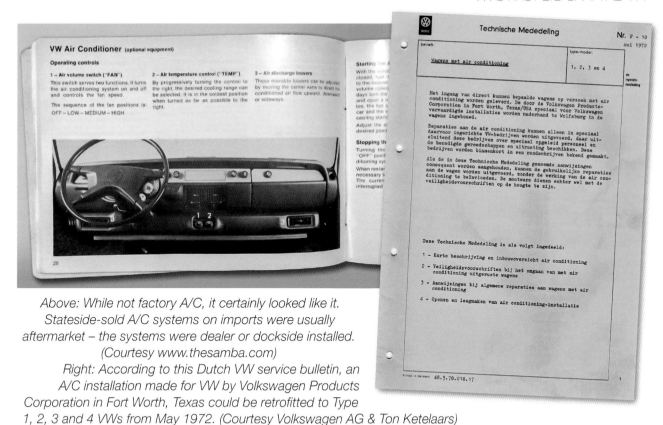

Above: While not factory A/C, it certainly looked like it. Stateside-sold A/C systems on imports were usually aftermarket – the systems were dealer or dockside installed. (Courtesy www.thesamba.com)
Right: According to this Dutch VW service bulletin, an A/C installation made for VW by Volkswagen Products Corporation in Fort Worth, Texas could be retrofitted to Type 1, 2, 3 and 4 VWs from May 1972. (Courtesy Volkswagen AG & Ton Ketelaars)

occupant injury, according to insurance companies like Folksam. Of immediate concern to VW engineers was rollover protection; so too, proximity of front vehicle occupants to the windshield. The concerns were related to proposed federal legislation, that never happened.

Fears over possible laws that would make the North American sale of cars illegal were enough to end the run of the VW Thing: the Type 181's windshield was too close to the driver and front passenger. Fortunately, the 1303 Bug's curved windshield solved this problem. In fact, the 1303's new age safety dashboard was designed to accommodate dual front airbags – something congressmen were mulling over as a future mandatory, or optional, passive restraint system.

It never eventuated, but, with all the legislative possibilities, it was planned

for. GM even made dual front airbags an option, on their 1974-76 full-size luxury models. The Type 4 411 was up-to-date concerning current and pending safety measures. With unitary construction it was easier to design progressive, collapsible crumple zones, and VW certainly did. Even though it wasn't an issue in Europe, the 411 was one of the safest cars in its class. In this respect it was on a par with the Volvo 144, and upscale Rover 2000.

The Type 4 was the most powerful VW launched to date. Aside from going, it was also none too shabby at stopping. In the past VW had done very well, with its well sized four-wheel hydraulic drum brakes. So much so that in January 1971, *Road & Track* said the Datsun 510 resisted fade so well, its disk/drum system was nearly as good as the Super Beetle's four-wheel drums! Well, North America never got

Available as a two- and four-door sedan on '69 MY debut, the 411's wagon Variant would have to wait for '70 MY. (Lutz Gaas)

The 411.

a Bug with front disk brakes. However, Europe did, starting with the Beetle 1500s of 1967. That said, all Type 4s came with generous 11.1in front disk brakes, and 9.8x1.78in rear drums. The stock brakes were non-boosted, and, in a 2500lb car with front disks, that implied a generous pedal shove to get some stopping action.

411 CREATURE COMFORTS
Disk brakes usually dissipate heat more rapidly than drums. However, when it came to a VW interior getting heat, the subject had been a long-term issue. It's so much easier with a conventional heater core that taps warm coolant from the radiator/cooling system. The worrying part was the fact that air-cooled VWs had no radiator. Once again, the Type 4 utilized traditional VW engine compartment

As with most air-cooled VWs, the Type 4 relied on the spare tire's pressurized air to work the windshield washer system. So remember to check that spare! (Courtesy Dan)

heat to warm the passenger cabin and demist window glass. It was exhaust system heat, derived from a heat exchanger and engine-driven cooling fan, through hoses. The 411 brought the refinement of an electric fan to boost low rpm heat supply.

The heat, and fresh air, came to the interior via a contemporary dashboard design. That meant slots cut out near the windshield, and face level fresh air vents. The latter would have been expected on any modern car from the late '60s, but was a newcomer to VW life, and very effective. A two-speed electric fan assisted flow-through of fresh and heated air. A stale air extraction slot was visible on the T4's rear C pillar. Ventilation slots in front of the windshield hinted at the presence of fresh air ventilation. Given fresh airflow through ventilation, the 411

eliminated side window vent wings. The higher cruising speeds of modern cars saw designers wishing to get rid of side panes that provoked wind noise.

1969 411 advertising mentioned a slight scoop on the upper edge of the front windows – this allowed draft-free ventilation, while keeping thieves at bay. However, the biggest news for comfort with the Type 4 was the gasoline-fired Eberspacher BA4 heater. The principle involved was gas being drawn into the heater, where it was vaporized and burnt using a large sparkplug. The result was instant heat – very useful on cold mornings before the engine had time to build up enough heat to supply the usual VW heating system.

Being an auxiliary piece of hardware, the Eberspacher worked

In Europe the 411 Variant was an alternative to station wagons, like the Peugeot 504 and Volvo 145. However, the VW was limited to two doors and a liftback. (Courtesy Dale Clow)

independently of the car's engine, and could be used to preheat the 411's interior with the engine turned off. A green dashboard warning light let the driver know the Eberspacher was working. A timer shut the system off, before the auxiliary heater could use too much of the gas tank's contents. Said gas tank had a capacity of 13.2 gallons (US), and the maximum duration was ten minutes. Even with the 411, the traditional VW engine compartment-derived heat supply let in a lot of engine noise. This made the Eberspacher device appreciated for its speed and quietness.

The gasoline heater was standard equipment on North American Type

North American buyers were hollering for a small, compact wagon, and the 411 Variant delivered. In North America, the AMC Hornet Sportabout arrived earlier in the '71 MY. (Courtesy Dale Clow)

4s, and Deluxe European models. On left-hand drive cars so equipped, an extra battery was placed under the front passenger seat. The 411's main battery, on left-hand drive cars, was under the driver's seat. With an Eberspacher right-hand drive version, the main battery would be under the front passenger seat, with the supplemental battery under the driver's seat. This was all part of giving the 411 better weight distribution, compared to regular VWs. Normally with VW, you would locate the battery under the rear bench.

One could also find an Eberspacher on some VW Type 181s. It was optional in some markets, standard in others.

However, on a Type 181 or Thing, the gasoline heater resided in the main luggage compartment. Not wishing to impinge on the 411's monster 400-liter frunk, a key selling point, the engineers placed the Type 4's Eberspacher above the rear transaxle. In spite of a rear window deckplate access aperture, the 411's gasoline heater was a real bear when it came to practical access maintenance (that is, unit removal, repair, or replacement). It's also true that the Eberspacher gasoline heater hoses deteriorate with age, and can leak. With the attendant heat in this location, leaking gas isn't good. In addition, replacement hoses from VW haven't been available for many years, so replacing them would be a custom job.

The flipside of heat would be the cold of an air-conditioning system (a/c). Air-conditioning was usually only seen on very expensive cars in Europe, in the Ferrari and Mercedes class. However, in America it was commonplace from an early time, and on more modest conveyances. By the mid '60s it wasn't uncommon to find a/c, either factory or aftermarket systems, on a humble domestic compact. With great relevance to VW, the rear-engined flat-six air-cooled Corvair had a factory system that placed the condenser over said flat-six: an odd arrangement considering condensers radiate heat. Given that air-cooled motors like an engine compartment as cool as possible, placing a heat dispensing condenser above said motor was unusual.

Imported European cars of the '60s, mainly upscale jobs like the Pagoda-roofed Mercedes SL, had aftermarket under dashboard a/c systems, that were either port or dealer fitted. The popular shovel-nosed Toyota Corona even had a factory set, that put its

blower box and vents in the glove box location! Japanese imports, and increasing buyer desire for a/c in economy cars, saw the Bug more frequently fitted with a/c from the late '60s. Although VW didn't factory-install a/c until the Dasher/Rabbit era, they did increasingly make provision for it.

The 1971 model year Super Beetle had slots cut into the front lower valence panel, in preparation for the car's optional a/c system. The North American handbook of later 1303 Bugs even had a page showing a/c fitted, and how to operate the a/c controls.

The Type 4 was slightly wider on the outside than the Super Beetle: 64.3in versus 62.4in. However, by going to unitary construction, compared to the traditional VW platform chassis, it made for a real roomy 411 ambiance. (Courtesy Dale Clow)

More than that, when Henry Manney took a look at the 1971 VWs for *Road & Track*, he mentioned the option 'Air by VW.' Well, the North American Type 4 handbook had an a/c page also. Once again the presentation suggested 'factory air,' but like anyone ordering a/c on their Bug, the system was fitted by a contracted installer at the port of delivery. The hardware was also American sourced, including an oversized York a/c compressor more suited to a small block V8.

It seemed engineers at Wolfsburg were mindful that people in America would be fitting a/c. This was especially the case in Southern California, itself a long time imported car mecca, and provisions were made to ease the installation. One purple and black wire in the T4's wiring harness was for the a/c compressor's clutch. The wire went from the dashboard to the engine compartment. Look to the left side by the relays on T4 sedans, and by the electric heater fan of Eberspacher equipped Variants.

A pre-stamped indentation on the

1972 Type 4s had the new four-spoke VW safety tiller, and the ergonomic benefit of a column stalk-actuated windshield washer/wiper. (Courtesy Dale Clow)

left rear sheet metal pressing could be utilized for an outlet elbow or service port concerning the a/c compressor. To run an a/c compressor off the motor using the usual belt method, a spacer between the flat-four's cooling fan and hub on the crankshaft could be removed. One could then run a pulley belt between the fan and hub. Four holes on the left end of the cooling shroud could aid in mounting a compressor. Furthermore, a stamped indentation on the right forward side of the trunk wall, slightly forward of the right wheel well, would help with the mounting of a fender well a/c receiver dryer flask.

Once again, looking at VW's M prefix option and accessory codes, the impression is given of factory items. The 411's a/c system denoted M573, and the later 412's optional a/c as code M705. However, the systems weren't installed at Wolfsburg. Given just about the only buyers considering the option were in America, it made dollars and sense to install it at the port of entry. VW's port-installed a/c systems were around two thirds the price of the factory systems, offered on comparable Japanese and domestic cars.

On the 411 and later 412 there was a shelf added below the dash with two outlets at each end of the dash. Two dials in the center controlled on/off/blower speed, and temperature. It looked an awful lot like Texan company COMFY-KIT's 'Factory Air' system from the late '60s. However, aside from this and an American compressor, VW a/c went its own air-cooled way.

It's relatively easy to fit an a/c system to a conventional front-engined car. The majority of the hardware is in a compartment in front of an interior, where the evaporator core lives. The two entities are connected by short

Reclining buckets with a good range of manual adjustment were one reason to buy an imported car, as opposed to American compacts. Independent rear suspension was another 411 comfort trump card. (Courtesy Dale Clow)

refrigerant hoses, with the condenser in the car's nose. In a rear-engined air-cooled car, it can be hard working out where to place the hardware. There is a convoluted refrigerant line path, with condensers (more than one unit per car) and drier flasks possibly winding up in fender wells.

The Type 4 had a serpentine a/c condenser, placed within the front lower valence. Instead of a conventional condenser resembling a radiator, the T4's unit was long and slender. It had two four-blade 8-amp condenser fans to the left and right of the spare tire well, below the trunk. Hot condenser air was pulled by the fans from the rear of the condenser, and exhausted under the car. Not an ideal arrangement concerning condenser fans, but space constraints left little choice.

The 411 didn't do badly, featuring a serpentine condenser when most cars had the simpler tube and plate fin style. However, going to a more modern parallel flow condenser, more suited to CFC-free R134a refrigerant, is a challenge due to finding space. Unfortunately the modern condensers come in the usual radiator shape, not something slim that will fit within the front valence. On a Type 1 or Type 3, a conventional condenser can be mounted above the transaxle. On a Type 2 Bus it could go under the vehicle, there is enough ground clearance to keep it safe.

On an American Type 4, with standard Eberspacher and the large 003 automatic, the transaxle location isn't possible. In addition, the 411/412's 5.3in ground clearance, makes mounting the unit under the car risky. Porsche 911/912s often use more than one aftermarket condenser, located in the fender well. With the

Type 4 this isn't really feasible, since the Eberspacher gasoline heater hoses live in the rear fender well. However, the Type 4's spare tire well may provide a custom option.

A hole could be cut in the bottom of the spare tire well, to mount a small auxiliary conventional aftermarket condenser and fan. A metal plate divider above, and vents for heat extraction cut in the aft end, would be a route to extra condenser capacity. Indeed, the Type 4's original optional a/c had the condenser unit in the spare wheel well. However, the spare could still be accommodated within said well! A plastic cover over the condenser, allowed the spare to still be there.

With climate under control, chances are seating comfort in the Type 4 was golden. The front seats of Deluxe versions were height adjustable, reclinable, and possessed three-position lumbar support. The last quality was a big Volvo sedan selling point at the time. 411 ads boasted that you could get three six-footers in the back seat, due to a flat rear passenger compartment floor.

It was the sort of argument front-wheel drive cars made: no troubles from having the big driveshaft tunnel, associated with a conventional rear drive machine. In the 411's case, the amenable accommodation was facilitated by an engine placed aft of the axle line. If there was a fly in the ointment, it was Volkswagen Group's penchant for placing the car battery under seating.

On the Bug and Audi 100, the battery was under the back bench. The respective reasons for the battery position on these two vehicles were space and weight distribution. With the Type 4, getting to the battery meant unlocking the driver's seat, and folding it backwards to gain access. On right-

Like a front drive car in reverse, the Type 4's rear-engined layout made for an almost flat rear floor. So the 411 could better accommodate three rear seat passengers than most American intermediate sedans. (Courtesy Dale Clow)

hand drive 411/412s, the place to look was the front passenger seat, and vice versa concerning the auxiliary battery for Type 4s with Eberspachers. In either case, access wasn't easy. The eccentricities continued with the 411's windshield washer system; this also held to VW tradition.

HAVE YOU CHECKED YOUR SPARE?

On a conventional car people would expect a plastic bottle filled with fluid, and an electric pump to get that fluid to the windshield via hoses and nozzles. However, the Beetle's simple utilitarian nature had eventually led to the air from the spare tire serving as a fluid delivery force. Why use a fancy electric pump, when you have all that pressurized air going to waste? So it was that Bugs, Karmann Ghias, Things and Type 3s used this ingenious system. The T2 Bus involved pressurizing the system with an air pump. In spite of the Type 4's rarefied, executive sector aspirations, it too used that front-mounted spare tire to squirt cleaning fluid.

One long hose traveled between windshield washer reservoir and washer nozzles, the other hose went to a special valve, the valve stem of the frunk-mounted spare. The owner was supposed to over-inflate the spare to 43psi, to provide washer fluid squirt power. A special valve in the washer reservoir's cap, would stop the tire pressure falling below 26psi. This way, one could still safely utilize the spare, under any circumstances. With age, the system could develop air leaks at the valve stem or hoses, and it was wise for owners to keep an eye on spare tire pressure during regular maintenance inspections. Then again, electric pumps can fail too. Naturally, VW's water-cooled cars utilized

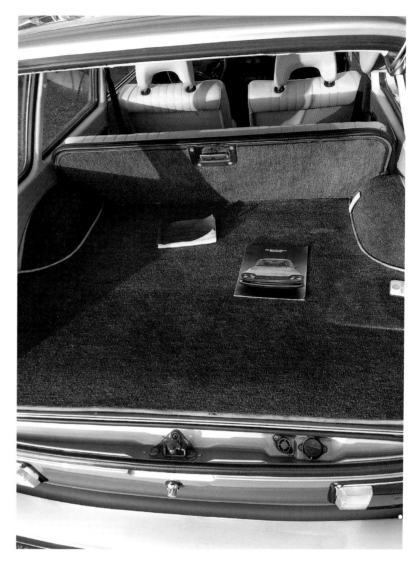

conventional electric pumps. Along with front-wheel drive, transverse engines and a hatchback format, these features were becoming the norm that European buyers increasingly favored.

Although the desire to go conventional, marrying the British Mini's transverse front drive layout with the luggage-friendly hatchback, became stronger with each passing day, the world was initially enthusiastic and hopeful concerning the Type 4. It was thoroughly engineered in the Germanic manner, and brought logical improvements to VW life. The 411

At last, a VW with lots of luggage capacity. However, the late 1971 model year American Type 4 brochure made no mention of the 411 coupe. Only the four-door sedan and Variant were described. (Courtesy Dale Clow)

Metallic paint, fuel-injection, four-wheel independent suspension and 24/24 warranty. In Canada, a four-speed could be ordered on 411/412 four-door sedan and Variant, too. (Courtesy Dale Clow)

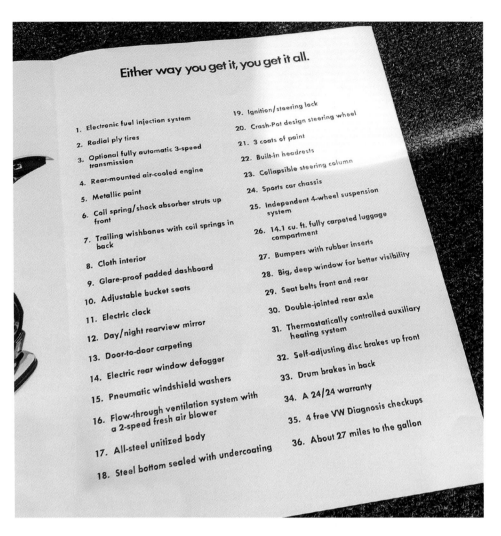

Either way you get it, you get it all.

1. Electronic fuel injection system
2. Radial ply tires
3. Optional fully automatic 3-speed transmission
4. Rear-mounted air-cooled engine
5. Metallic paint
6. Coil spring/shock absorber struts up front
7. Trailing wishbones with coil springs in back
8. Cloth interior
9. Glare-proof padded dashboard
10. Adjustable bucket seats
11. Electric clock
12. Day/night rearview mirror
13. Door-to-door carpeting
14. Electric rear window defogger
15. Pneumatic windshield washers
16. Flow-through ventilation system with a 2-speed fresh air blower
17. All-steel unitized body
18. Steel bottom sealed with undercoating
19. Ignition/steering lock
20. Crash-Pot design steering wheel
21. 3 coats of paint
22. Built-in headrests
23. Collapsible steering column
24. Sports car chassis
25. Independent 4-wheel suspension system
26. 14.1 cu. ft. fully carpeted luggage compartment
27. Bumpers with rubber inserts
28. Big, deep window for better visibility
29. Seat belts front and rear
30. Double-jointed rear axle
31. Thermostatically controlled auxiliary heating system
32. Self-adjusting disc brakes up front
33. Drum brakes in back
34. A 24/24 warranty
35. 4 free VW Diagnosis checkups
36. About 27 miles to the gallon

also promised excellent reliability and quality associated with the brand.

Looking at what VW had for '69 MY, *Road & Track* noted electric heated rear windows, anti glare rear view mirrors, plus no more swing axles for North America. However, the Type 4 seemed to offer wholesale rather than VW's usual piecemeal changes. The journal was moved to say, "… with nice stuff like the 411 coming right out of Wolfsburg these days, one cannot help but wonder just how much longer they can prolong the life of the archaic Beetle, healthy sales or not." Of course the Super Beetle had yet to arrive, but *R&T* observed that, technically, aside from a rear-mounted air-cooled flat-four, the 411 was a genuinely new machine, and held much promise.

411 MEETS
THE WORLD

The opening 411 ads asked the questions, "Does more Volkswagen mean better Volkswagen?" and, "How much more does more Volkswagen cost?" The Type 4 family first hit West German dealerships at 7700DM for the plain two-door, and 8165DM for the upscale 411L or 411 Deluxe. The four-door equivalents listed for 8090DM and 8485DM, respectively. In Belgium it was 96.900F for the two-door, 101.700F for the four-door. Complete in specification

The new 411 four-door at the Amsterdam International Autoshow on February 16, 1969. (Courtesy Dutch National Archives)

The two-door 411 joined its four-door brother as the Type 4's opening models. One could get a 1969 411 coupe in West Germany from 7700 Deutschmarks. (Courtesy Volkswagen AG)

though they were, especially the Deluxe editions, there were many ways to personalize a Type 4.

SO MANY OPTIONS

On the amenities side of things, the M603 Luxury Package included many items seen on the 411L: chrome wheel covers (M218), bumper overrider rubber strips (M58), rear mud flaps (M74), side parking lights, full reclining seats, fold out rear armrest, leatherette

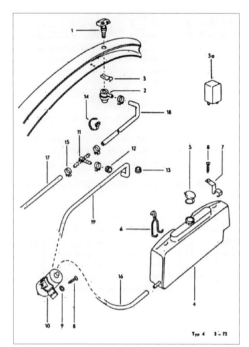

The M288 headlamp washer jet option was mandatory on Swedish-delivered 412s by 1974. By now, the associated electric motor was located under the windshield washer tank. (Courtesy Volkswagen AG & Ton Ketelaars)

upholstery, electric clock, cigar lighter, passenger sun-visor and vanity mirrors, dipping rear-view mirror, full carpeting, brake circuit warning lamp, and ignition switch with a steering column lock. In Europe 'leatherette' refers to vinyl, a term used on all makes, not just VWs. It was appropriate because well-done vinyl back then was much better than the low ball 'leather' you find standard on many regular, and not so regular, cars today.

411 cloth seats were coded M53. For a real touch of luxury back then, the sliding steel crank handle sunroof was coded M560. M430 and M244 accounted for the laminated front windshield tint band, and sedan rear window factory tint respectively. M93 and M98 took care of the pop-out panes for the 411 two-door and 411 Variant respectively. They were popular items on cars in the pre-'80s era to boost interior ventilation. M653 intermittent windshield wipers were once regarded as an upscale item. So too the factory issue push-button M95 'Wolfsburg' radio.

VWs had certainly moved on from the days of Bugs with optional flower vase holders. There were also several worthwhile mechanical options. To curb oversteer M103 HD (heavy-duty) shocks and M220 limited-slip differential were to the good. To reduce fade HD brake linings were M523, and M506 power brakes were advisable. The latter helped because, compared to drum brakes, disks have limited natural assistance. Therefore, even on a relatively light car like the 2500lb Type 4, pedal pressure can get excessive when hauling down speed. Halogen front foglamps (M659) and rear foglamp (M571) were handy, and even mandatory in some European countries.

The Type 4's fresh air/heating ventilation system was already much more than on VWs of yore. However, the M200 option code brought a bigger blower unit. Also fashionable with new European cars were headlamp washer jets, coded M288 and located in the front bumpers. There was a large washer water tank between the headlamps, and an associated electric motor. Force for the jets was too high to use the air pressure from the spare tire. Then, as now, if one was to tick many desirable option boxes it would make a dealer happy, but empty a bank account quickly. The days of the VW economy car were numbered.

An optional sunblind for the 411. As per other air-cooled VWs, an extensive range of factory accessories existed for the Type 4. (Courtesy Lutz Gaas)

A Lower Saxony VW 411LE patrol car: it was VW's home turf. In spite of economic restructuring away from manufacturing to the service sector, VW AG is still the biggest private sector employer in the state. (Courtesy Polizei Niedersachsen)

Five VW factories are located in Lower Saxony; so too VW's Wolfsburg headquarters. Plus, the state of Lower Saxony owns 20.3% of VW AG. (Courtesy Polizei Niedersachsen)

This 1971 411E Variant fire brigade 'commander's wagon' is a sole survivor, and still wears its original paint. (Courtesy Hilmar Walde)

The VW Type 4 was a siren call to VW fanciers wishing to live large. (Courtesy Hilmar Walde)

Emergency service vehicles came with radio gear installed, but the miniature model is a custom touch! (Courtesy Hilmar Walde)

It's appropriate that this Variant has the optional Eberspacher fuel burning heater. Just the thing to keep the fire brigade commander comfy! (Courtesy Hilmar Walde)

So much space, you could fit a Type 1 Bug in there. The 'V' in Variant stood for versatile … maybe. (Courtesy Hilmar Walde)

The use of MacPherson strut front suspension made for a commodious 'frunk' on the Type 4 and Super Beetle (1302/1303). (Courtesy Hilmar Walde)

While on duty, the fire brigade VW 411E passes a civilian contemporary rival, the Opel Rekord. Top right: On duty in Offenburg in the '70s. Even back then VW's Type 4 emergency services sales weren't big like Beetle. (Courtesy Hilmar Walde)

CHASING THOSE FLEET SALES

It seems VW wasn't just looking for private buyers with its 411. There were packages designed for usage by the police, emergency services, taxi operators and other fleet operations. The M613 Police Vehicle Package came with a blue revolving roof light, external loudspeaker and radio interference suppression kit. For your cop 411, one could enjoy an M48 police green leatherette interior. The M160 siren kit was applicable to police, ambulance and fire services.

The Type 4 was used by such government and law enforcement agencies, but not as much as other VWs or other brands of German car. For one, the 411 wasn't a cheap car, and Audi, BMW and Mercedes had the police pursuit end of things. West German police were big on the new 1972 Audi 80. Beetles and West

Type 4 versatility should have helped. However, a crowded and competitive market rained on Wolfsburg's parade. (Courtesy Hilmar Walde)

German Fords tended to cover more mundane police duties. That was the Type 4's problem in late '60s Europe, there were so many models to choose from. Even so, VW had something for taxis and other rental fleets that might have considered the 411. There was the M678 Rental Car Equipment Package, and the M533 anti-theft alarm system for taxi rental Type 4s.

WHO WILL BUY THE TYPE 4?

It's handy when you already have an established market. In 1968 VW was the undisputed economy car king with the Beetle. However, that was economy cars. The VW 411 was kind of like Maserati with its 21st Century Ghibli. A VW luxury car that entered someone else's territory? As VW's first big car, the 411 showed the trouble the brand would have in the years ahead, when trying to sell an upscale car with that VW logo. Whether it was the much later VW Passat W8, or the lofty ambitions of Ferdinand Piech concerning the VW Phaeton, even the acknowledged VW Group mastermind couldn't make the proverbial horse sup water.

VW's difficulty in this arena was also shown when launching the new, big third generation Passat in the late 1980s. Twenty years on, and with a car that also had a smooth, grilleless visage, VW was again in a quandary. How to explain a big, plush people's mobile? It was a consumer problem for a psychologist, if nothing else. Like the earlier Type 4 it had little to do with mechanical properties, or relative competitor performance. The solution for VW UK … was the 'Drop Ad.'

The Drop Ad was successfully utilized by VW in the UK to sell water-cooled era models. It was greatly associated with the Mk1 and Mk2 Golfs. So, it made sense to apply this ad style to the new Passat. Trying to bring the newcomer into clan VW, if you will. For a variation on the usual ad format, a Beetle, Polo, and Golf would be dropped at set intervals, with the TV presenter walking along as the cars hit the floor, and bounced a little. Then came the Passat, and being bigger it went through the floor!

The intention was to prove VWs were tough. So tough, you could drop 'em, and the new Passat was a VW, only larger. So big, it doesn't just bounce. The ad agency theory was sound, but VW still had a hard time

convincing prospects that they should journey to VW at this price point, with a large European car. In the public's mind 'Vorsprung Durch Technik' slipped off the salesman's tongue so much easier at the Audi dealership. It was the reason Toyota called the LS400 a Lexus, not a Toyota. Ditto Honda using the Acura brand and separate dealership network, to move upscale Hondas.

Similarly, even though the VW Phaeton could do Ferdinand Piech's bidding of 180mph plus, when it was 110°F outside and 72°F inside the Phaeton's plush, climate controlled cabin, meant little. The Phaeton was badged as a VW, and at this price level the answer was Audi A8. As with the VW Type 4, the hope with the Phaeton was to move VW's image upscale. It seemed like the People's Car image

VW was hopeful for Type 4 fleet sales. Indeed, a lack of four doors for taxi licensing requirements contributed to the Type 1 Beetle's Mexican demise. (Courtesy Lutz Gaas)

Apart from low volume CKD South African assembly, most VW Type 4s emanated from the Wolfsburg plant shown. (Courtesy Volkswagen AG)

didn't know whether to rhyme Audi's name with star Audie Murphy, or a Texan greeting, but the car still sold plenty. Many are still perplexed how Audi survived its reliability woes of the '70s, and *60 Minutes* TV show phantom acceleration troubles of the '80s and '90s. Ingolstadt did though, and went on to put the sales heat on former corporate masters Daimler-Benz. Sometimes you don't need an engineer, or someone from sales and marketing, to explain something … you need that psychologist again!

VW sales and marketing were having similar challenges, with the Type 4 at launch. How to let buyers know this was a new, upscale, luxury VW, without losing the VW faithful. The ads tried to play it both ways. One ad said, "It's more Volkswagen than you'd expect," and showed the Type 4's large four-door interior and cavernous frunk.

From humble first time exports with Dutch Opel dealer Ben Pon, the Type 4 brought big things for VW in Holland! (Courtesy Volkswagen AG & Ton Ketelaars)

was a tough one to shake. After all, *Road & Track* subtitled its first VW 411 test in February 1971, "A more affluent wagen for more affluent volks." How many volks? A fair number, but not as many as the car with the four ringed logo. The funny thing was, in the early days, many overseas buyers

This 1969 411 is a first year Type 4 with an early chassis number. A four digit VIN indicates a September 23 1968 build date. (Courtesy Lutz Gaas)

However, the UK ad assured prospects that this VW was a VW you already knew; it plainly said that although new, the traditional VW features were present: a 'no boil or freeze' air-cooled motor, rear engine layout for superb traction in slippery conditions, and bolt-on fenders, easier to install and cheaper than welding.

To put any doubts aside, the ad said the special VW attention to tuning, fit/finish, paintwork and final inspection checks, were still in evidence at Wolfsburg. To try and prove such claims, pictures of diligent factory workers were shown, appearing to care more than any UAW character you ever saw. A four-door 411 was also displayed with its right rear fender removed, to show both bolt on ease and VW quality. The main picture in the ad featured a two-door 411 sedan in profile. Given VW cars had only come

with two doors thus far, it was another reassuring sight that put the minds of the VW faithful at ease.

In spite of all the usual VW fare, the quality of strength afforded by unitary construction was emphasized. However, in 1968 this engineering item was harder for the average buyer to comprehend than a fancy styling job.

The 1969 411L was very well equipped in standard form. It came with radials, rear window defogger, and gasoline powered heater, at no extra charge. (Courtesy Lutz Gaas)

With unibody construction, MacPherson strut front suspension and Eberspacher gasoline heater, the Type 4 really brought something new to the Wolfsburg shindig!

The Big VW, that's what Wolfsburg's PR machine proclaimed the new Type 4 to be. This was true, but the initial oval headlamps did polarize styling opinion. (Courtesy Lutz Gaas)

In keeping with modern late '60s cars, the 411 eschewed vent wings. Fan forced flow through ventilation, and face level vents sufficed. (Courtesy Lutz Gaas)

Many of the aforementioned safety features of the Type 4 were mandated by the federal government. The buyer at large wasn't overly concerned with safety in the late '60s, especially if they had to pay for it. Indeed, the 411's safety qualities may not have been appreciated. Henry N Manney, of *Road & Track*, put the VW folks on the spot in Martha's Vineyard in late 1970. He simply enquired, who would buy the newish 411? At this North American press launch for the 1971 VWs, the VW people didn't really have an answer. They couldn't state specifically which demographic set would proffer their John Hancock to buy the 411, or which rival cars Wolfsburg hoped to challenge.

The situation revealed more about VW, than the Type 4. English designer Harris Mann, of British Leyland fame, revealed how focused Ford Europe was at the time. When he arrived at Dagenham to work on the European Escort, he was informed of Ford's objective. Make a car like the Vauxhall Viva, but do it more cheaply! The lack of a clear public goal for the 411 led to statements like those from Manney, that by 1970 the 411 had "… laid sort of an egg in Europe." Without clarity from VW, public and critics looked upon every new model VW released as a Beetle successor. When the new car didn't sell at Beetle volumes, it was immediately branded a failure.

The critic's mindset was typified by *Car and Driver*'s view of VW and the pending 411, "Wolfsburg seems to have decided that all it has to do is build a bigger Beetle and the world will continue to beat a path to its door – we're wondering if that path might not be detouring to the Far East." Amidst the confusion, the critics and public mixed up the 411 with the Beetle. All VWs were the same, with *C/D*

The latter was the stock in trade of VW's Continental rivals, Ford Europe and Opel (GM Europe). One couldn't option a vinyl roof on a VW. However, dual circuit brakes, collapsible steering column, soft plastic dashboard controls and radial tires were standard. In addition, separate colored taillight segments, one per function, were a touch of class. When so many domestic cars merely extinguished lights on one side, or went dim, such technical superiority was a sign of thinking and fewer bean counters at Wolfsburg.

considering the 411 more evolutionary than revolutionary.

MADE IN WEST GERMANY AND ...

The fact remains that the Type 4 sold for around 50% more than the average Beetle, so by having the 411/412 around, it was like selling an extra 100,000 Bugs per year. In addition, if buyers were detouring from VW to the Far East, they were also surely taking that route away from other European and American automakers. The Japanese weren't just scoring conquest sales from VW: this was also related to where the Type 4 would be built. Apart from Wolfsburg, there was also assembly in the right-hand drive market of South Africa.

To escape high import duty the 411/412 and other VWs were assembled by VW Suid Afrik. However, given the smaller market, they had to be selective with model versions offered, to achieve economies of scale.

In 1969 it was possible to buy a 411 two-door sedan or upscale 411L. The 411 four-door was only available in Deluxe trim, and could have automatic transmission as the 411L Automatic four-door. Through local assembly it was possible to have a 411 two-door four-speed starting price of 2120 rand. In South Africa it was billed as 'The Big Volkswagen,' and an assurance was given that the motor was still in the back and air-cooled.

The South African ad said, "There are some things you just can't improve on." Indeed, the 411 offered luxury touring at a VW price. In the rugged, hot lands of South Africa, air-cooled VWs made sense. However, in reassuring the VW faithful that it was still business as usual, Wolfsburg was possibly selling the 411 short. The Type 4 had so much that was genuinely new, but ads that restated VW tradition created the idea of the same old VW. It also invited Beetle sales comparisons.

That longer 98.4in wheelbase was new to VW cars. However, was the 411 VW's future family car? (Courtesy Lutz Gaas)

If you want even more rear accommodation in a VW ... buy a Type 2 Bus! (Courtesy Lutz Gaas)

It was better to sell the 411 short, than not at all. With driving conditions like South Africa, there were also plans to assemble the Type 4 in Australia. VWs had been successfully assembled Down Under since the 1950s. The Beetle's air-cooled nature, and rugged torsion bar front, swing axle rear suspension, had proved very adept at dealing with an arid land where many roads were unsealed. The roads that weren't much good either. However, things had changed coming into the 1970s. Being tough was no longer enough.

Pre-dating America's experience of the late '60s to early '70s by around three years, Japanese imports had stolen many sales from the locally assembled VW Beetle. More standard features, comfort and lighter controls, plus better roads, aided the rise of Toyotas and Datsuns. Indeed, it was Nissan that took over VW Australia's Clayton, Victoria plant in 1977. Nissan would continue Australian production of their cars to 1992. Long before all this, there were plans to make the revised 411E four-door in Australia, both in automatic and manual transmission forms. To gauge the public's appetite for such a car, several

The absence of a passenger side exhaust marks this 411 sedan as a non-Eberspacher Type 4 car. (Courtesy Lutz Gaas)

411s had been brought to Australia for evaluation.

There was a belief that a basic model, could successfully be sold around the $3000 AUD level. Such plans were made in anticipation of the updated 411E and 411LE, to be shown at the 1969 Frankfurt Autoshow. Possible Type 4 assembly could have been done by Motor Producers Pty Ltd, such was newspaper speculation. This firm had also been doing Datsuns and Mercedes trucks locally. Apart from the Beetle, the VW 1500 (Type 3) was already in Aussie production, in manual and automatic forms. This was done according to an annual 7500 unit production plan, which required 60% local content under Australian law.

The Type 3 Notchback, Fastback and Squareback 1600s, were also produced according to a 2500 unit annual scheme needing 40% local content. Ambitions by VW Australasia to get into the 7500-25,000 unit bracket, had been curtailed by economic reality. VW sales had been falling with Japanese and local (Ford Australia and General Motors Holden) competition, making the high 90% local content unrealistic. It seemed Australia and the rest of the world increasingly wanted conventional cars. This trend was occurring even before the coming of front-drive hatchbacks.

As in South Africa the motivation for local assembly was to avoid exorbitant import duties. Money for the government and a desire to protect the local car industry. With VW's sales volume on the slide, the Australian operation sold its stamping machines and foundry, so large scale production of the 411E wouldn't have been possible anyway. In 1972 LNC had also brought in a few right-hand drive Type 181s for evaluation. However, it was judged commercially difficult for this off-roader to compete with the locally made Mini Moke. Therefore, the VW Thing didn't make it Down Under.[7]

A 1969 UK market RHD 411 in Essex. Could Wolfsburg wrestle sales from upscale Austins, Fords and Vauxhalls in the British Isles? It proved difficult. (Courtesy Charles)

The news, back in late 1969, was that there were plans to import the Audi 100 and the 'Volksporsche.' The latter 914 was described as VW-financed and Porsche-designed. There was a view the 914 would compete with the MGB, leaving the upscale 914/6 to contend with Alfa Romeo coupes. However, the lack of a factory right-hand drive 914, made the Fourteener cost uncompetitive as

a sports car in Australia. It was another sign of the changing fortunes for Volkswagen.

Wolfsburg in the late '60s, seemed to have the products and the answers. Better stuff than the company was offering when the Beetle was in its '50s and '60s heyday. The 411's aluminum cases were tough enough to be repaired, welded and even align bored safely. The Type 4 had a lot of sound material added, compared to earlier VWs. In addition, the Type 4 had redesigned intake and exhaust manifolds, directed at improving refinement. Four-speed T4s even featured hydraulic clutch actuation, not cable as per earlier VWs. However, changing circumstances and rival manufacturer competition, made for a hard road ahead for the 411 and VW.

THE AA CALLS VW'S 411!

There was great interest in VW's new Type 4 from car magazines, drivers, industry analysts and automotive groups. This included the UK's AA

The Type 4 was significantly upscale for a VW: a 1970 411LE Variant is shown. (Courtesy Volkswagen AG)

(Automobile Association), with this motoring body examining the VW 411L in 1969. They noted that in its home market, the Type 4 was a VW response to ever ritzier rides from Ford Germany and Opel. For British buyers, the AA judged the 411L as the most comfortable and sophisticated VW to date. Aside from the familiar rounded styling, immaculate finish and rear motor clatter, the AA said the Type 4 brought much that was new to VW.

Although not a fast car, and purposely set up for high speed cruising, the AA said, "... acceleration is by no means sluggish." Overall fuel economy tested out at nearly 26mpg (UK imperial) on low octane two-star gas. They found the new Type 4's four-speed a trifle notchy into first, but fast and precise elsewhere, with excellent synchromesh. Handling was judged VW's best yet, with zero propensity to oversteer. However, ride comfort proved bouncy when the going got rough.

The windshield wipers hadn't been converted to right-hand drive style, and the heater was judged ineffective, unless the Eberspacher was employed. The AA measured the latter's gasoline consumption, at up to a pint per hour. For Britain, exterior Type 4 colors were beige, blue, red, green and white. Base sticker for the 411L was £935 and 18 shillings. Weekly total costs, including depreciation, were stated as "nine and six", to use the UK's pre-decimal vernacular.

The AA's journal also provided the experience of AA member and London resident Terry Edwards. Mr Edwards used his 411 four-door as a main family car. He had owned VWs since being stationed in Germany with the armed forces. His opinions and experiences concerning German cars, and VWs in particular, echoed UK views of the day. Edwards only non VW ownership episode involved a British-built and designed Ford Cortina. He noted that the Cortina represented the only time that he had to call on the AA for roadside assistance.

In 1970 Europe, the 411LE sold for the equivalent of $2900. Road & Track's Henry N Manney said target market and early sales were sketchy. (Courtesy Volkswagen AG)

Edwards' favorite VW quality was terrific reliability. The Type 4's styling and ample interior space also rated a mention. The 411 owner considered his previous VW, a Type 3 Fastback 1600, as possessing superior off the line acceleration. However, he felt the 411 was much more stable in crosswinds. Edwards also liked the slow revving 411 1700's effortless ground covering ability. He didn't find the 411 noisy, but acknowledged that others did.

TYPE 4 – 1970 REVISIONS

The interest in Audi in the premium sector market, had meaning for Volkswagen in the near future, and much further along too. The desire to sell something Porsche-related was also telling. In West Germany, VW outlets had been selling Porsches as a sideline for years, but come 1970 this would change. In the '50s and '60s, VW had a positive association with Porsche. It revolved around like-engined cars, with a common design origin. However, with Audi in the ascendancy, and a move to separate Porsche from VW, old ties were being lost. Indeed, Audi and NSU would have a commercial bearing on the Type 4's success.

Not unlike VW's ad for the 1971 Super Beetle, so many changes were made to the 411 for 1970, that they were starting to show. Critics said the appearance revisions were in response to lackluster sales. Either way, the

oval headlamps of 1969 were history, at least as far as deluxe 411s were concerned. They were replaced by equal sized pairs of round lamps.

If anything motivated the change, it was a need to accommodate American lighting laws, commensurate with a plan to export the 411 to North America. However, that plan took longer than expected. Earlier on the '69s had the VW logo on the frunklid, black rims and aluminum trim rings. In 1970 the badge moved to the 411's nose, and there were silver rims, but no trim rings. 1970 also saw horizontal chrome bars flanking the nose logo. Chrome beauty trim also circled the pairs of round, equal sized headlamps. In this era, having pairs of round lamps was considered an upscale, sporty touch.

Road & Track's Henry Manney judged the Type 4 Variant as a pretty good looking unit in its own right. However, station wagons, or three and five doors as they were called outside America, majored on practicality, not looks. Here, the three door only 411/412 Variant scored well, having a maximum cargo capacity of 1380 liters with the rear seats folded down. VW's lower profile T3 and T4 flat fours made for a practical load area. The semi-trailing arm rear suspension helped too. An American 1971 VW ad suggested that the Type 4's load area could serve as a children's rumpus room. With a thought to safety, hopefully the 411 Variant would be stationary when this was tried.

Adding to the frunk capacity produced a total Variant load-lugging capability of 1780 liters. With North American buyers on the lookout for a smaller, more maneuverable station wagon to replace their over 200in-long domestic intermediate 'Chariot of the Gods.' The boxy, but not really

The Minichamps (400051101) scale model of the 1970 VW 411LE. (Courtesy Kharon8)

This is a 1970 model year VW 411LE in original Pastel White, color code L90D. (Courtesy Hilmar Walde)

With VW badging, 'L' stood for deluxe and 'E' for fuel-injection. (Courtesy Hilmar Walde)

foxy, 411 Variant was a more sensible 178.1in long, prior to impact bumper times. Doubling one's gas mileage with adequate performance was nice too. To achieve this result, VW had a new version of the Type 4's 1700 motor ready for 1970. The latest powerplant

explained the 'E' suffix on the 1970 411E and 411LE's tailscript. Injection starts with the letter 'E' in German (einspritzung), and 1970 Type 4s had Bosch D jetronic computer controlled fuel-injection.

This fuel-injection system was

Mit dem Komfort einer Luxuslimousine.

Der neue VW Variant 411 E hat den gleichen Komfort wie die Limousine.

Auch er hat bequeme Einzelsitze vorn. Mit Längs- und Höhenverstellung. Sogar mit vollverstellbaren Lehnen.

Und bequeme Rücksitze. Auf denen drei Personen Platz haben, ohne daß sich ihre Füße ins Gehege kommen. Denn es gibt keinen Mitteltunnel.

Damit die bequemen Sitze auch bequem zu erreichen sind, hat er große Türen.

Und damit es schön warm wird,

wenn es Ihnen zu kalt ist, können Sie die thermostatisch geregelte Heizung einschalten. Die auch dann warm sein kann, wenn der Motor kalt ist.

Oder Sie können sich Luft machen. Durch die zug- und geräuschfreie Frischluftanlage. Mit Zwangsentlüftung im Heck.

Dazu hat der VW Variant 411 E eine gepolsterte Armaturentafel. Sicherheitstürgriffe. Und eine sorgfältig verarbeitete Kunststoffverkleidung.

Sie werden sehen, daß Sie ähnliches in einer Luxuslimousine nicht immer zu sehen bekommen.

Many US VW enthusiasts would have loved to have seen the four-speed available on Stateside Type 4 sedans and Variants. (Volkswagen AG)

Electrojector was never fitted as a regular production line Rebel option. Bendix stopped development, and then licensed the Electrojector system to Bosch. For the time being, fuel-injection made little headway in the USA. Gas was cheap, pollution control wasn't an issue, and it was cheaper

and easier just to use bigger V8s for a few more horsepower.

In the '60s, various mechanical injection systems were used on sporty, upscale European cars. Kugelfischer (BMW), Lucas (Triumph) and Bosch (Mercedes) setups were all available in some world market. These were mostly indirect systems, the Bosch setup seen on Mercedes cars was the best known internationally, and had a plunger-style injection. However, once again something new lay on the horizon: Bosch D-jetronic from Volkswagen. The Electrojector wasn't dead; Bosch took the early computerized system as a starting point for its D-jet system. It was the world's first modern, volume produced, computer controlled fuel-injection.

Many parties in America and Europe were working on injection systems in the '60s, but it took Bosch and VW to introduce a reliable, cost effective fuel-injection system of the kind seen on all modern cars.

Und deshalb haben wir mit dieser Konzeption auch einen VW Variant 411 E gebaut. Mit 80 PS.

Mit dem Fahrwerk eines Sportwagens.

In the early '60s, 80 PS was Porsche 356 1600S territory. So, VW was right to dub the injected Variant a sports wagon! (Volkswagen AG)

Für Leute, die noch größere Ansprüche an einen Wagen stellen. Und bereit sind, dafür etwas mehr Geld auszugeben. Der VW Variant 411 E hat einen Motor mit elektronischer Benzineinspritzung. Dazu alle Annehmlichkeiten einer Luxuslimousine. Und die Nützlichkeit eines Geschäftswagens.

Es ist ungewöhnlich, daß ein Wagen mit dieser

Konzeption ein so aufwendiges Fahrwerk hat.

Mit einzeln aufgehängten Rädern, die sich unabhängig voneinander der Straßenoberfläche anpassen. Mit Federbeinen vorn. Die Stöße und Schläge so abfangen, daß Spur und Sturz immer konstant bleiben. Mit einer Schräglenker-Doppelgelenk-Hinterachse, die

den Wagen auch in scharfen Kurven sicher abstützt. Und serienmäßig mit Gürtelreifen.

Außerdem hat der VW Variant 411 E eine selbsttragende Sicherheitskarosserie. Mit Knautschzonen. So daß sich bei einem Aufprall der Vorder- und Hinterwagen zusammenschiebt und den größten Teil des Stoßes schluckt.

A Swedish spec 1970 411LE two-door is displayed. They didn't just drive Volvos and Saabs out there! This car was specified with extra 'frunk' carpet and head restraints. (Courtesy Lars Sellbom)

To achieve this, Bosch drew heavily on the Bendix Electrojector patents. However, D-jet's design details and engineering were all Bosch. Pairs of injector nozzles fired simultaneously, with this intermittent system, there were also tuned length, ram induction pipes courtesy of Wolfsburg's intake manifold design. D-jet sensed intake manifold vacuum pressure changes to create an electrical signal relayed to the computer brain via a potentiometer.

The so called computer 'black box' was, in reality, a silver case the size of a cigar box. It lived on the left-hand side of the engine compartment in the Type 4's example. The computer observed the signal, and worked out the duration the injector solenoids would remain open. The term injector is misleading – with fuel-injection a high pressure electric pump forces fuel along, from the gas tank to the injector solenoid. The solenoid screen door opens, and out comes the fuel into the inlet tract.

Working at 24-30psi, the D-jet system was too high pressure to allow the formation of vapor in the fuel lines.

That is, the dreaded vapor lock of carb engines. However, high pressure mechanical systems, like the Bosch plunger system on Mercedes W108 250/280SE sedans, or Kugelfischer injected BMW 2000/2002tii, worked at far higher pressure. They were mainly set up for high-performance, not pollution control. There was no 'chip' in the D-jet system that could be programmed for more horsepower, it was an analog setup. However, American Volvo tuner IPD did an early form of chipping for the D-jet injection

Thanks to the Eberspacher, you didn't need to fear a VW interior when the going got cold. Four on the floor made the VW 411LE even more lively. (Courtesy Lars Sellbom)

seen on Volvo 140/160s in the early '70s.

For 75 bucks in 1974, IPD added a manual controller dial, whereby the driver could adjust the air/fuel mixture on the fly. Going from 10% lean to 30% rich in increments of 5%, one could simulate a removeable EPROM chip. By going rich for autocrossing and circuit racing, or lean for highway cruising, the system was flexible. Where could Bosch D-jetronic fuel-injection be found? On the 1968 Type 3 1600s, and the 1970 Type 4 411E, and same year Mercedes small block V8 sedans and convertibles. In 1970 D-jet also found its way to the Volvo 1800E sports car, and the 1971 Volvo 144E sedan. For 1972 it arrived on the Euro spec BMW 3.0Si sedan and 3.0CSi coupe.

Historical records show VW was the first to put Bosch D-jetronic, on a volume made production car. In 1968 North American motivation, as per Daimler-Benz with their mechanically injected rides, was to get around the nation's inaugural pollution laws, sans the indignity of smog pumps, transmission controlled spark and the

like. In fact, VW confided in 1968 that it could have gone for more power and better economy, with their new injected 1600, were it not for federal pollution laws. As it stood the 1600 made 65bhp at 4600rpm and 86.8lb/ft at 2800rpm on a 7.7:1 CR. The carb 1600 produced 60bhp at 4400rpm and 82lb/ft at three grand on just 7.5:1.

The gains for respective carb and injection 1700s were 68bhp at 4500rpm and 91lb/ft at 2800rpm on 7.8:1 CR, versus 80bhp at 4900rpm and 97lb/ft at 2700rpm on an 8.2:1 CR. Factory figures for the 411 carb manual and automatic, were a respective 90mph/0-62mph in 18 seconds, and 88mph/0-62mph in 21 seconds. For the injected 411E manual and automatic, the game had moved on to a respective 96mph/0-62mph in 17 seconds, and 94mph/0-62mph in 20 seconds. However, the real gains here were in the 411's behavior with fuel-injection.

With the coming of emissions controls, cars had difficulty starting and with general running until warmed up, and sometimes not even then. Often it took two tries to start, followed

The 80 horse Bosch D-jet Type 4 motor with long intake runners was shared with the 1970 VW-Porsche 914. (Courtesy Lars Sellbom)

The Type 4 was much more rust resistant than the German Ford Taunus or Opel Rekord. Rust doesn't respect fashion. Side marker lights and rubber strip bumpers were factory options. (Courtesy Lars Sellbom)

It may have looked like a hatchback, but it was a two-door sedan. The right exhaust pipe on Type 4s was for the Eberspacher heater. (Courtesy Lars Sellbom)

by a high idle speed, and stumbling due to lean carburetion. Even when warmed up a car would surge, and be tricky to drive at a constant speed. *Road & Track* had these problems with a Mercedes 280 compact, tested in its February 1973 issue. The journal pondered why Mercedes didn't import the injected version, given that the 280 was so difficult to drive. In contrast, cars like the Type 3 1600 and Type 4 411E (the 'E' part was omitted from the American market designation) were a piece of cake.

The VWs started first time without touching the gas pedal and could be driven away immediately sans stumbling or surging. When it came to good drivability and meeting pollution law, fuel-injection was essential. GM was a domestic leader in smog control drivability, but wasn't in this league of no fuss, no muss driving. However, fuel-injection was an expensive item not available on most cars, including Bentley. Just as well VW Group bought them out, to help 'em out! VW/Bosch injection allowed performance levels to be maintained as emissions got tighter. Those tuned intake runners helped fatten the torque curve, too.

Standard fitment of pricey fuel-injection on the VW 411E made this near luxury car very good value indeed. Even so, with any newly-introduced technology there are doubts. *Road &*

Track noted that while its 411 sedan performed with aplomb, failure of the ECU would be expensive outside warranty. In addition, many mechanics regarded fuel-injection as nothing less than pure witchcraft – they didn't wish to deal with it, since they had limited or no experience with injected cars. Well, VW had the situation covered. At a time when many cars had a mere six month/6000 mile or 12 month/12,000 mile warranty, air-cooled VWs were on a 24 month and 24,000 mile bumper-to-bumper warranty. Speed shops offered just 90 days' basic warranty on early Camaro 427s!

VW also offered four free diagnostic inspections concerning 411, and the fuel-injection tied in nicely with VW's low maintenance, computer diagnosis offered at authorized dealers. Since so few cars in the world were available with Bosch D-jet, Bosch could keep a close eye on quality, and avoid the disposable nature of 21st century ECUs. The 1970 411E/LE shared its injected 1700 flat-four with the new VW/Porsche 914. Indeed, that car's concurrent development and shared basic suspension layout has prompted Type 4 authority Judith Rastall to suggest the 914 be thought of as the Type 4 roadster!

Radical thinking perhaps, but with the 914 and 914/6, Volkswagen Group was going for an image bridge akin to the Fiat Dino and Ferrari Dino: from VW 411LE to 914 and 911, a seamless transition from Wolfsburg to Zuffenhausen, care of Osnabruck (Karmann). The 411E and 914 had fuel-injection, but the upscale Audi 100 did not. Ingolstadt devotees had to wait until the CIS mechanical system of 1976 model year. Worse than that, the Audi 100 also came with Audi drivability, which wasn't too special.

At the core of the Audi's 'Middle

With fuel-injection and a wagon Variant for 1970, the Type 4 had qualities not even the upscale C1 Audi 100 could boast. (Courtesy Volkswagen AG)

Fuel-injected 411LEs being completed at Wolfsburg. In total, 367,728 Type 4s were built between 1968 and 1975. (Courtesy Volkswagen AG)

Pressure' OHV inline four pot was a high compression ratio. Naturally, America's smog law mandated a compression ratio drop for 1972. This was at variance with the Middle Pressure philosophy. Running on from this was the Audi designed Fox powerplant. This unit would also cause woes, with early carb Dashers and Rabbits, experiencing poor drivability of a most annoying manner. In contrast, VW's laid back flat-four was already in a low state of tune. Many don't realize, that there was no fall in rated horsepower between Euro and US market flat fours. In addition, the 411E was able to retain its 8.2:1 CR when it went to the American market.

The ability to run on low octane gas was held in common with Porsche powerplants. However, when the 411 reached North America, its engine was listed as requiring premium gas. Then again, in Continental Europe the Type 4 M599 option code listed the carb 1700 as being available, until the end of 1973 model year. At this point all European Type 4 motors reverted back to carbs. For 1972, the UK market 411LE was the sole version available. North American Type 4s were always fuel-injected.

SIBLING RIVALRIES – AUDI & NSU

The Type 4's life was never going to be easy, it had rivals outside of and inside the VW Group. An unexpected quasi rival came in the form of Ingolstadt's Audi. During 1958-64, Auto Union was owned by Daimler-Benz, and in 1958 the Stuttgart luxury car maker acquired 88% of Auto Union shares. Daimler-Benz also helped with the establishment of a new factory, where the next generation of Auto Unions would be made. These cars would have a lot of Mercedes influence, and a Daimler-Benz influenced inline four. As things stood in the DB era, the sole surviving postwar member of the once illustrious Auto Union was DKW. This company was familiar for making front-drive, two-stroke powered automobiles. Mercedes' plan for the future, would mainly happen for VW and Audi.

It seemed DKW shared the VW

VW got Audi when it bought DKW from Mercedes. Audi and the 411 were part of VW's upscale plan. Here, Hidemi Aoki poses with a MB 320SL. (Courtesy www. facebook.com/pg/swissmotorsau)

Type 4's bad luck. DKW's new Mercedes-backed design, the F102, was launched with the usual two-stroke engine. German buyers were becoming more affluent, and wanted a four-stroke powered car. In 1965 the F102 was rebranded an Audi under VW ownership, and, with its intended Middle Pressure engine of Mercedes influence, was a commercial success. However, the true purpose of VW's DKW acquisition was merely extra production capacity for the very hot-selling Beetle.

Another important asset VW got from the DKW purchase was Mercedes engineer Ludwig Kraus. VW management was happy to see new, improved versions of F102 badged as Audis. However, the top brass told Kraus not to do any clean sheet Audis. In 1965 Beetle production began at the Ingolstadt factory, 61,830 VWs and 52,207 Auto Unions were made at the Audi factory that year. Ludwig Kraus heard what management had to say, but went about designing a new Audi anyway!

Former VW of Brasil boss Rudolf Leiding was now in charge of Auto Union (Audi). One day he noticed the Kraus prototype as a clay model in Ingolstadt's styling department. Leiding thought it was great, and, to get around VW management's new Audi model freeze, designated the Kraus prototype as a body modification of the F102. VW

The 411 surprised the VW faithful with four doors, and everyone else with standard features that were either options, or just plain unavailable on other upscale cars. (Courtesy Volkswagen AG)

management was invited to inspect Kraus' work, and was as impressed by the design as Rudolf Leiding was. VW supremo Heinz Nordhoff was particularly impressed – perhaps a little too much – and VW management decided there and then to make the car … as a VW!

Audi's boss Leiding was able to persuade the top brass that it would be wiser to produce the car under the Audi banner. So it was that the design proceeded as project Type 104, and became the first generation Audi 100, the C1 of 1969-76. The new 100 was a further commercial hit for Audi, and was made alongside an expanded F102 based family until 1972. At this point the F102 cars gave way to the all new Audi 80, or Fox. It was early in 1967 that Heinz Nordhoff had permitted development of a new front-drive, medium sized car coded EA272. This would become the Audi 80 and Passat (Dasher).

Not only was the new 80 yet another business triumph for Audi, it was a critical success too. Indeed, the car garnered the 1972 European Car of the Year title. Audi was on a roll; by 1969 600 Audis were being built per day. With European demand for Audis greatly exceeding supply, VW production at Ingolstadt ceased. The world just couldn't get enough of Audi! So it was that in 1973, the one millionth Audi came off the line at Ingolstadt, since the marque's 1965 restart. What was happening here was that Volkswagen Group had accidentally discovered that buyers everywhere,

To overcome high import duties, the Type 4 was incorporated into VW Suid Afrik's local assembly program. This made for a competitive starting price of 2120 Rand. (Courtesy Volkswagen South Africa)

The VW/Porsche 914E shared injected 1700 took the VW 411E four-speed on to 96mph. Like all air-cooled Vee Dubs, the Type 4 could do this top speed all day long! (Courtesy Volkswagen AG)

A South African assembled 1972 411L Variant is shown. (Courtesy www.thesamba.com)

were hungry for a third prestige German brand.

The rise of Audi with the 100 was kind of like Lexus with the LS400 20 years later. There was a bunch of consumers ready for a certain product. However, unlike Lexus the success for Audi kept coming. That Audi had the Midas touch was also apparent from its American success. In spite of lacking automatic transmission and factory a/c, the Audi 100 made a smooth and cool start. In TV and print ads it was billed as "A lot of car for the money." This was because, in such ads, the new Audi brand and the 100 was compared to the Rolls-Royce Silver Shadow, Caddy Eldorado and Mercedes W108 280SE.

It was the traditional comparison ad meets *Lifestyles of The Rich and Famous* and *Dynasty* combined! The Audi had the traditional, conservative three box Mercedes-like styling to pull it off. No surprise here, given Daimler-Benz earlier ownership of Auto Union. Naturally, the VW Type 4 couldn't be promoted in such upscale fashion. The 411/412 were advertised in a more downbeat way.

The sentiment with VW ads was more 'we know it's unusual to have

This is a 1970 411 four-door sedan. There was much speculation about when exactly the Type 4 would reach America. Early reports said '70 MY. (Courtesy Volkswagen AG)

a VW this pricey, but bear with us because it's actually a good car.' Given the VW badge, the Type 4 couldn't be compared to glamour rides, nor share the trappings of Blake Carrington. In the 1980s Joan Collins owned 25 Rolls-Royces, simultaneously! If you can't afford a Rolls-Royce or a Mercedes, don't worry, you can have an Audi.

Further good fortune on Audi's part was its front engine/front-drive layout, just like an Olds Toronado and Caddy Eldo. At the moment the Audi reached America, front-wheel drive tech was seen as the height of modernity. To add insult to injury, the Audi 100 arrived in America a year before the VW Type 4. The 411 made its American debut with automatic transmission and fuel-injection standard. It would be another five years before the Audi 100 could offer such features together to North American buyers. Even then, the Audi's automatic was optional.

The VW 411 ads didn't talk about megabuck imports, they compared the 411 to the solid, dependable Beetle. Probably not the way to win over professionals like doctors,

lawyers and dentists. Then again, with the VW badge was this even possible? Utilitarian values don't usually accord with upscale luxury touches. Little wonder that by the '80s Audi's 'Vorsprung durch Technik' and BMW's 'The Ultimate Driving Machine,' were slaying yuppies in the wine bars. Meanwhile, in the words of *MotorWeek*'s John Davis, Cadillac was burying customers by the cemetery's worth!

It seemed American buyers believed the Audi's upscale ads. In contrast to

Här finns det plats

1.780 liters bagageutrymme. I Volkswagen 411 LE Variant har man 1.380 liter bakom förarplatsen och under huven fram finns plats för ytterligare 400 liter bagage. Och detta i en vagn med personbilskomfort! Ingen dålig rymdbil — eller hur?

With 400 liters of 'frunk,' plus 1380 liters with the rear seating folded down, the Type 4 Variant was a load lugger of uncommon capacity. (Courtesy Volkswagen AG)

Enthusiasts modify their Type 4s like any other VW. This 1972 411 Variant sports a four-speed stick and 1.8-liter 914 motor, with dual Weber ICT34s and Scat camshaft. (Courtesy Robert Curtis Huffstutler)

the view of rear-engined, air-cooled cars, many thought the Audi 100 was the way to the luxury car future. *Road & Track*'s Henry Manney noted that his cousin Margaret fell for the Audi 100LS he was using, while awaiting his '73 VW Sports Bug test steed. At this family gathering, the Audi's sunroof garnered considerable praise. However, something funny happened on the car carrier, transporting Audi 100s and Foxes to the New World.

For one, Audis were sold at a super premium price in America, even relative to their upper middle class European position. Secondly, the cars had enough reliability and quality control snafus to sink the Bismarck! High on the gripe list hit parade was the Audi 100's inboard front disk brakes. Designed to reduce unsprung weight and improve handling yes, but also a maintenance nightmare. The car's electrics were also a concern. Many an owner may have been moved to check

if Audi was a subsidiary of British Leyland, and not Volkswagen, so troublesome were said electrics.

Somehow, Audi weathered these stormy seas, and even more in the '80s. The '70s Audi Fox was no bastion of trouble-free driving either. In a *Road & Track* owner survey from a 1976 February issue, only 70% of Fox owners said they would sign their John Hancock for another Audi. Fortunately for Audi, finding first time buyers was so easy, they didn't have to sweat over the repeat custom. It's all about the sunroof … Meanwhile, there was evidence to show VW was having a hard time charging a premium for Wolfsburg's finest.

Type 4 ads went to great lengths to justify the 411/412's price. They itemized the standard hardware and comfort features that one received with the Type 4. It was something established market sector rivals didn't have to do. The ads showed that the

Straight cut cam gear and race trim low back seats show sporting Variant intent. Lowered suspension, BMW 17x9in alloys, and a relocated battery are further functional modifications. (Courtesy Robert Curtis Huffstutler)

411 and 412 buyer got a lot for their dough. However, that People's Car stigma was hard to shake. The issue was brought up, even when a VW wasn't at hand. When testing hopped up Novas and Darts for *Cars* magazine in July 1974, Joe Oldham took aim at the '70s phenomenon stagflation. He noted that folks were signing away their pay packet on four grand Bugs.

What's wrong with spending more money on a well made, better specified version of the People's Brand? VW had little difficulty moving Sports Bugs and Grande Bugs. However, buyers did and do have trouble processing the idea of a VW costing more dollars. An Audi was pricier, but a VW was expensive. Whatever happened to the old saying of something only being expensive if it didn't work? In any case, Audi was now on the scene. It set up an interesting dynamic in model planning and development within the Volkswagen Group.

There was a consideration to building the Audi as a VW, and having another division at VW, influencing which VWs would be released. Among the design proposals considered at VW in the late '60s was an Audi motor at the front, in a front or rear drive car coded EA259. A trial of the front-engined, front-wheel drive prototype of EA259 was the deal maker or breaker concerning the Type 5, or VW 311. As it turned out, the test went negatively, and this possible Beetle replacement that Heinz Nordhoff and others had held out so much hope for, bit the dust.

Over time the Type 5 project had fallen behind schedule, and as of February 1969 it was officially cancelled. VW decided to go with a revitalized Type 3 range for 1970 instead. However, a revised version of this near-decade-old range was no long-term solution. The Type 3 would draw to a close at the end of 1973 model year. Indeed, in such tumultuous times, the fact the T5 had fallen far behind schedule helped give the T4 411 a shot at production. Yet another wildcard in the 411's baptism of fire was the arrival of NSU in the VW Group.

Successful small German company NSU was big on motorcycles and

In this see-through illustration of the reworked Type 4 412E, the fuel-injection ECU (silver box) can be seen to the left of the 1700 motor. The Eberspacher heater lives above the transaxle. (Courtesy Volkswagen AG)

The 'black box' was really silver, and the electronic brain of the Type 4's D-jetronic fuel-injection used in 1970-73. (Courtesy Volkswagen AG)

Inside the silver box of the Bosch D-jetronic, computer-controlled fuel-injection was fitted to some Type 3 and Type 4 Volkswagens. (Courtesy Volkswagen AG)

small cars. With the latter it was the rear-engined, air-cooled Prinz. The Prinz was like a mini Chevy Corvair in layout and looks, but handled and sold well. Indeed, over 800,000 were sold by the early '70s. However, NSU is best remembered for its attempts with, and licensing of, the rotary engine. Yes, that Felix Wankel marvel that no one except Mazda seemed to get right. In the February 1968 issue of *Wheels*, journalist Pedr Davis recounted his trip to NSU's werks at Neckarsulm.

In spite of the staff and management being optimistic, Davis sounded a cautionary warning. He noted the tremendous investment NSU had made in the rotary powerplant. NSU as a small specialist, like Mazda, saw rotary as a survival plan in a world of auto giants. Pedr Davis wrote, "It will take, I think, a full three years before the company's shareholders will know if they are travelling into greener fields or off the map altogether."[9] As it transpired, it would take much less than three years.

It's now a matter of recorded history that NSU's rotary engine, and the Ro80 it was featured in, didn't really make it. The car and the concept were brilliant, coincidentally, like the later Audi Fox, another front-drive European Car of the Year, this time in 1968. However, problems with excessive rotor tip seal wear, saw the Ro80's rotary engine in frequent need of replacement. The cost of said replacement engines under warranty was more than NSU could financially take. In the end, just 37,204 Ro80s were built by the time production ended in 1977.

NSU tried to improve rotor tip seal durability, and some claimed its engine longevity improved over the years. However, the sedan still attracted the joke title of Raw80 in Germany, due to the lack of preparation in the car's development. Long before production ended, NSU was forced into a merger with Auto Union. At a difficult shareholder meeting it was agreed in 1968 to sell 59.5% of NSU shares to VW. In 1969 VW, Auto Union and NSU agreed to the creation of Audi NSU Auto Union AG. However, why buy a moribund automaker?

VW was the majority shareholder in the new combine, and there was method to their madness. VW were desperate to have a front-wheel drive, water-cooled model in their portfolio, and NSU had one. NSU had created a piston engined counterpart to the

This 1972 Bahia Red VW-Porsche 914 was delivered with the factory options of extra sail panel black vinyl, and Pedrini alloys. (Courtesy Lars Sellbom)

The 914's 80bhp 1.7L, fuel-injected Type 4 motor was used in the VW 411E. (Courtesy Lars Sellbom)

rotary NSU Ro80, called the K70. Piston in German starts with the letter 'K.' The new front-drive, water-cooled K70 shared some engineering and styling with the NSU Ro80. However, in contrast to the semi-automatic only Ro80, the K70 was a manual transmission only car. In addition, neither NSUs were officially sold in North America. So, there were two qualities distinguishing it from the VW Type 4.

The K70 was never produced as a NSU, it was launched as a Volkswagen, with great hope from the Wolfsburg concern in 1970. Like the NSU Ro80, the VW K70 was an upscale sedan. Suspension was all independent, like the Type 4, but aside from the VW badging the K70 shared no parts with any other Volkswagen. That included the 1605cc SOHC inline four-cylinder. The car was conventional looking, but subjectively quite ordinary in appearance. It was somewhat of a cuckoo in the VW nest. Between 1970 and 1975 210,082 VW K70s were sold. Later examples featured a 100 horse 1.8-liter inline four, giving 100mph. Once again, very close to the VW Type 4 412 of the day.

Many in America considered the 1970 Audi 100 to be the luxury car of the future. Here, Hidemi Aoki is with the 2018 Audi RS5. (Courtesy www.nepoeht.com)

COMPETITION FROM ALL SIDES

Judged somewhat uncharismatic, the VW K70 was seen as only a moderate sales success, and was mainly sold on the Continent. If the new Audis and K70 weren't enough, then there was also the arrival of the VW Passat in 1973! A well known nameplate internationally, and available in North America with automatic transmission from the start. It arrived for 1974 model year, and was a truly successful water-cooled, front-drive Volkswagen. A herald of the company's future indeed. VW had engaged in what the British, BMC, used to be accused of, badge engineering. Dr Kurt Lotz's successor Rudolf Leiding, former Audi boss, had seen how well his new Audi 80 had done. He wisely decided that a VW version of said Audi would be timely.

So it was that the Audi 80/Fox was reskinned into the VW Passat/Dasher. Evidence of the shared background came in the North-South orientation, of the Audi designed inline four pot. The Dasher was water-cooled, front-drive, and a hatchback would be available

The fuel-injected four-door 1970 411E on the Wolfsburg line. West German leaded Super Benzin gas was 98 octane, and 'sinfully expensive,' as the Germans like to say! (Courtesy Volkswagen AG)

for '75 MY. The Passat's Achilles heel in America, and the same applied to other new age Audis and VWs, was that Audi inline four.

Audi motors didn't take kindly to North American smog equipment, and low octane gas. They didn't behave in a civilized fashion on carbs. In contrast the traditional VW air-cooled flat-four was a laid back, low compression motor that could drink any gas grade. This all forced a crash program of Bosch K-jetronic fuel-injection adoption, to get the Audi motor to run properly. In the Dasher's case, one had to wait until 1976 model year.

As an emissions control side note, NSU had got their Ro80 Wankel powerplant emissions ready for '72 MY. However, by this stage NSU's reliability woes were starting to bite hard back home. Unfortunately, the Ro80 never got officially exported to North America. It would have met its Waterloo with tighter emissions regs, and federal impact bumpers, even if it had managed to circumvent the Wankel's rotor tip seal wear bugbear. As the Dasher, the new Passat soon became a commercial force to be reckoned with. Like its soon to be Scirocco and Golf brethren, it was one of the few European imports that didn't resemble a defaced Mona Lisa, when impact bumpers came along.

The Passat/Dasher was like a VW Type 3 replacement, but with the added versatility of a four-door sedan, and four-door hatchback or five-door in European parlance. However, the Type 4 also offered four doors, and this proved to be yet another source

This is a Gemini Blue Metallic 1970 411LE Variant automatic. It was the most expensive Type 4 one could purchase. (Courtesy Dr Aiken Brent Krahmer)

The sport rims and mudflaps are some of the genuine VW accessories added to this Variant. These items include US spec red taillight lenses. This Variant was originally sold by West German dealership Lohmann, which was in business from 1933 to 2010. Factory mudflaps join commonly seen US spec VWoA items like bumper overriders and roof rack. The Italian market front turn signal lenses are a rarity. Chrome bezel headlamp surrounds are on everyone's VW 'unobtainium' list these days. Headlamp stone guards and pop-out side windows all hail from the VW accessory catalog, and this Variant's got 'em! (Courtesy Dr Aiken Brent Krahmer)

of internal VW Group competition. The VW K70 had four doors, so too the Audi 80 and 100. Before 1969 VW never made a four-door car, now it had several, and so did many European rivals. With the recent arrival of Audi, NSU and new wave Passat, the Type 4 had its work cut out. In racing, the first guy you want to beat is your team-mate. In some ways VW had become a German British Leyland, with several models fighting over the same piece of road.

Looking at the price levels of the respective models, where available in one market, there was certainly a pricing hierarchy, akin to that at GM, Ford or anyone else. In this game the Passat was the most inexpensive way to four-door land at camp VW. It might be assumed this would keep the larger Type 4 safe. However, the '70s phenomenon that was downsizing was alive and well on both sides of the Atlantic. To combat higher gas prices, rampant inflation and even insurance premiums, the Type 4 prospects must have considered the Passat/Dasher.

By the end of 1974 model year, all contenders were present in the UK market. Cheapest was the Passat LS four-door at £1466. *Autocar*'s 1.5-liter example did 98mph and 0-60mph in 12.4 seconds and 27.8mpg. The next cheapest comparable four-door in the VW family was the Audi 80GL at £1594. On test it did 101mph, 0-60mph in 11.5 seconds and 34.5mpg. The VW 412LS four-door was £1605. By this hour the Type 4 was on 1.8 liters, with factory figures of 98mph and 0-62mph in 14.5 seconds. The earlier fuel-injected 411 four-speed tested by *Motor*, managed 23.5mpg overall.

Higher up the price charts came the VW K70, an also 1.8-liter sedan but costing £1674. It was the most expensive VW model sold. *Autocar*'s

The Type 4, as the 411LE, joined a Japanese market VW lineup that included the Super Beetle and Karmann Ghia. (Courtesy Volkswagen Japan)

figures for the NSU design were 93mph, 0-60mph in 12.9 seconds, with 24.1mpg overall. Back to planet Audi with the 100LS at £1841. Figures for this model were 106mph, 0-60mph in 11.9 seconds and 23.7mpg. The very adventurous, by 1974, could have tried the most expensive VW Group four-door, the NSU Ro80 retailing at £3018. This three-speed semi-auto Wankel wonder produced 107mph and 0-60mph in 13.9 seconds. It was the thirstiest of the clan at 18.2mpg overall, and the world was just getting over the first fuel crisis!

All the above concerned basic list prices, and UK mpg economy figures. It's apparent that VW Group had a wide choice of near luxury and luxury class contenders. It also seems true that the Type 4 may have lost out sales to the cheaper Passat, the more conventional looking K70 and the prestige sector Audi brand. Perhaps the only model that wouldn't have challenged the 411/412 in sales was the much pricier Ro80. There was a belief at this time, that when a manufacturer introduced a smaller, cheaper line, it would cannibalize sales from an existing larger, higher priced line. This certainly seems to have happened with the introduction of the Passat.

The subcompact Passat/Dasher seemed to achieve conquest sales from the larger compact sized 412. There was also the modern phenomenon of buyers preferring a smaller luxury brand car, instead of a larger non prestige model. So on both sides of the pond buyers were tempted by the Audi 80/Fox, away from the bigger 411/412. However, reliability troubles caused many to regret that move. With such interfamilial competition, it's understandable why the Porsche+Audi franchise started in North America in 1970.

There were cases in America, where buyers wanted the new smaller Dasher, but were swayed by dealers towards special deals on VW 412s. Such special pricing on remaining air-cooled stock like 412 and VW Thing in '74 MY was promoted in ads. They had to do some convincing, given

The compact-sized Type 4 was unlucky to be introduced during the early '70s North American explosion of interest in subcompacts. (www.thesamba.com)

the mass desire for front-wheel drive hatchbacks. A look at the sales figures for the aforementioned VW Group models helps explain where the money went, and how successful different brands were. The Type 3 amassed 1,813,600 unit sales in 1966-1973, with the original Passat/Dasher on 1,769,700 between 1973 and 1980.

The similarities in figures between the Type 3 and Mk1 Passat, lends credence to the thinking that the former was replaced by the latter. Like the Type 3, the Passat started with a 1500. Both subsequently went on to 1600 power. Up the price charts the T4 family garnered 367,728 sales between 1968 and 1974. Upscale of Type 4 was the VW branded K70 with 210,082 units from 1970 to 1975. Around the Type 4's upscale price position, the physically smaller Audi 80/Fox chalked up 939,931 sales between 1972 and 1978, as a Mk1 model.

The further upscale prestige Audi 100 family, including Coupe, got 827,474 C1 based sales between 1968 and 1976. The priciest member in VW Group land, the NSU Ro80, earned 37,204 customer conquests from 1967 to 1977. The figures help explain where VW Group was going. The route was basically front-drive, conventional and prestige. Indeed, when production of the Ro80 drew to a close in the summer of 1977, the second generation Audi 100/5000 C2, took its place at the NSU Neckarsulm werks. With the Audi 100 C2 being a front-drive executive car, taking on series 2 BMW 5 series, and the Mercedes W123 Compact, also revised for 1977, the Audi 100 C2 was seen by many as the Ro80's successor.

The subsequent aero Audi 80 B3, possessed many design elements of the NSU Ro80, while lacking the NSU's exciting design and engineering

This 1972 411 Variant has the practicality of a small family wagon. Boxy is foxy!

Like the similarly-named Porsche 911, a familiar smooth, whirring boxer tune could be heard aft of occupants. (www.thesamba.com)

detail. No more NSUs were produced after 1977. Audi effectively took over the Neckarsulm marque's prestige position. Commercial success of the four ringed logo, showed this to be VW Group's prestige avenue of choice. During the time of the NSU Ro80's ascendancy, Mercedes and BMW responded to the Wankel challenge, by saying it felt prestige buyers in the European 2-liter class would favor a proven, reliable and conventional design. It seemed Audi's success affirmed their belief. In 1985 VW Group revised the Audi NSU Auto Union AG name, to simply Audi AG.

VW'S NEW SALES WORLD
In the lower price classes, it should be noted, the coming of the plusher, more practical Super Beetle stole some sales away from the VW Type 3. In comparison with the Passat, the VW Type 3 range was stronger saleswise than many have judged.

At the local VAG (Volkswagen Audi Garage) VW Golf GTi and Scirocco would soon complement a line up of prestige Audis. The practice of including Porsche too, persisted in some export markets into the mid 1980s, like the Middle East. However, such old ways were fading. In 1985 it became no longer possible, to buy a new Beetle in West German VW showrooms. Between 1978 and the mid '80s, Beetle supply had come from VW do Brasil.

Volkswagen AG without a Beetle? It was a thing many thought would never come. In this new age VW started becoming a middle class, glamor brand in Europe, thanks to that GTi cachet. It also became clear that selling a sedan needed a prestige badge – handily, this job was taken by Audi. For a time cars like the European Ford Granada/Scorpio and Opel Omega/Vauxhall Carlton still sold well. However, getting into the 1990s saw non prestige sedans swapped for MPVs in Europe and SUVs in America.

By the time Ford Europe and Opel gave up sedans, the market for big Fiats, Lancias, Citroëns and Rovers had long gone. This trend towards a car type without a market was experienced early by the VW 411/412. Regardless of solid design and mechanical virtues, the majority of buyers were staying away from ordinary brand sedans. It had been recognized that European buyers followed a consumer guide direction, more than brand loyalties. In America there was more brand loyalty, but price was always important.

It was assumed VW would have an automatic market for the Type 4, or any diversified product it offered. That is, Beetle owners wanted something to trade up to, while remaining loyal to their trusted brand, with its extensive parts and service network. There were indeed dyed-in-the-wool VW faithful, that were pleased with a wider range of models, with more gadgets and plusher interiors. However, it seems many Beetle owners were economy car buyers first, and VW owners second. They bought Beetles because at that price level, it was the right choice for reliability, quality and more. That said, if they had more money, they would look at a pricier model of any brand, not necessarily a pricier VW.

There was also a worldwide trend where German cars became associated with high-performance (VW Golf GTi), prestige (Audi 100) or both with the 1980s Audi Quattro. However, an air-cooled family car, with a design connection with the increasingly distant Porsche marque, was becoming a harder sell. During the Type 4's final year, Audi launched the sports oriented Audi 80 GT. This sports sedan accorded with the new global view of German cars much more than the end game VW 412s, or even the much loved Karmann Ghia.

A CHALLENGING
ROAD TO THE 412

It still seemed to link back to the good Doktor, since the view of German cars as resembling sports luxury was increasingly galvanized by the high profile, internationally admired Porsche brand. Could a German car be any other way?

The '70s was the era of the car mantra. It was said imported cars were terrific and domestic cars were completely terrible. There was a belief that the C3 Corvette was junk, and should have been replaced after week one by that advanced, mid-engined sports car enthusiasts had been promised since the dawn of time. It was also thought rear-engined, air-cooled cars were old hat. The Beetle was seen as a poster child for the past. The way to the future was front-drive and water-cooled. Anything that didn't comply just wasn't modern.

MEET THE PRESS
The thing with mantras is that if you say them often enough, they start to become the gospel

Volkswagen announces a new kind of Volkswagen. Big.

Who'd ever believe it? A Volkswagen that's big. And looks like a regular car. And has four big doors. And more room and comfort than you've ever seen in a Volkswagen. And more power and acceleration than you've ever had in a Volkswagen.

From the most powerful engine we've ever put in a VW. (But our big car goes about 22 miles per gallon.) And has more features as standard equipment than you'd ever expect to find in a big car. Like an automatic transmission. Radial tires. Front disc brakes. Electronic fuel injection. Rear-window

defroster. And more. So now, after all these years, you can buy a big car as good as our little car. The new 411 Volkswagen Four-Door sedan. You know what? You just ran out of excuses for not buying a Volkswagen.

"A big car as good as our little car," said VW. The 411 automatic went twice as far on a gallon of gas, and offered the same or more interior space as that of an intermediate V8. (Courtesy Volkswagen AG)

It's possible the conventional looks of the prototype 1966 Type 4 notchback might have garnered more sales amongst the conservative, sedan-liking, family car class. (Courtesy Charles)

truth. Automotive publications and industry commentators initiate such pronouncements, and soon the general public sings along too. It made it difficult for the new Type 4 411 to get a fair hearing. At the model preview stage *Car and Driver* said something about the VW 411 being a big Beetle, and the great unwashed making a beeline for Datsun, Toyota and at a pinch, Fiat. Esteemed West German journal *Auto Motor und Sport* followed along similar lines.

The German car magazine featured the up-trimmed VW 411L in their 1969 issue, putting the new VW up against its European competition. The field

involved the Fiat 125, Renault 16, old DKW design Audi 80L, Ford 17M and Opel Rekord 1700L. This was a big deal, given the 411 was VW's first new car since the Type 3 1500 of 1961 vintage. More than that, Volkswagen was the company more than most associated with West Germany's rise from the rubble of World War II. How would the now affluent German middle class judge VW's latest car, as the company and country were about to enter the 1970s?

Auto Motor und Sport judged the new 411 harshly, putting the Type 4 last in the group test. This was even harder for VW to take, given the plush 411L was the most expensive car Wolfsburg made, and the priciest car on test. The magazine's conclusion suggested its reporters had approached the encounter with anything but an open mind. They dismissed VW as stubbornly clinging to tradition, and not looking at what was going on in the outside automotive world.

The cars on test were either familiar, conventional or admired. The Fiat had all those things the motoring scribes love. A twin-cam 1.6-liter inline four, four-wheel disk brakes, some versions with a five-speed even. The Fiat 125 wasn't an all new design, but managed 603,870 sales between 1967 and 1972. Over the same period Ford of Germany's 17M had an OHV V4 of 1.5 to 1.7 liters and 723,622 sales.

A contemporary of the Type 4, the Opel Rekord of 1966-72 also had four coil suspension, but a single overhead cam I4 of 1.5 to 1.9 liters. Opel sold 1,280,000 including six-cylinder editions. The front-wheel drive camp, saw in-house competition from the ex DKW F102 based Audi 80, and the Renault 16, both model families started in 1965. The Audi and Renault had OHV inline fours, but the Audi had the Mercedes sourced Middle Pressure trick, and Renault had its lightweight all alloy motor.

After years of the unconventional, rear-engined, rear-drive Renault 8 and 10, Le Regie had gone front-drive and front-engined with the Renault 16. In addition a spacious hatchback body was added. This model lived on to 1979, reaching a total of 1,846,000. From this field alone, it can be seen VW was entering a hotly contested segment. There would be no free lunches given, concerning conquest sales. To make things worse, from 1970 model year, Renault added the also front-drive Renault 12 sedan.

The Renault 12 was a three-box sedan, so too the Fiat 125, Ford 17M and Opel Rekord, plus Audi 80. However, the Fiat, Ford and Opel utilized a live axle rear suspension. The Ford 17M still had leaf springs. However, Europe's Ford and GM subsidiaries employed American-look styling. This was worth showroom gold compared to the Type 4's unconventional style. It was easy to overlook the fact VW 411 had independent, semi-trailing arm rear suspension. It also had build quality that lasted much longer than one Italian summer. VW and Renault avoided the space wasting nature of a driveshaft tunnel. However, VW offered the modernity of a console shifter, not the Renault 16's column change.

It could also be said that while some of the above would go on to feature mechanical fuel-injection, none had the Type 4's electronic, computer controlled injection. Unfortunately, the Type 4's fuel-injection would only arrive in its second year. Germany's Rainer Guenzler took a close look at the new 411, in basic two-door sedan form. The VW 411 was pitted against its usual foes. Guenzler was a well known sports journalist, TV host and racer. In *Der Spiegel Autotest* No 135 he put the 411 two-door through its paces on

Electronic VW diagnosis and four free inspections helped keep your VW on the road. The dependability wasn't new, but the Type 4's size and comfort were. (Courtesy VAG (UK) Ltd)

the track. Here he derived oversteer, understeer and Swiss neutrality from the 411's unibody chassis.

On bare figures VWs have never shone that brightly. That's because air-cooled VWs were set up for durability, with their maximum speed coinciding with their cruising speed. It should also be remembered that VWs were capable of running on lower grades of gasoline compared to rivals, due to their lower compression ratios. Air-cooled VWs would also maintain good gas mileage figures when driven hard, at high speeds. Rivals would perform at their best if drivers pretended there was an egg under the gas pedal. With VWs the rate of economy drop off with more exuberant driving wasn't as sharp.

With all of the above in mind, the basic 411 two-door matched its *Autotest* rivals from Opel and Renault quite closely. Bearing in mind 10 liters of gas per 100km is roughly 23.5 USmpg, the 411 two-door four-speed with 68 horses managed 147km/h, 0-100km/h (0-62mph) in 17.4 seconds and 12.2-liters per 100km for 7700DM. The Renault 16

1500 with 55bhp reached 146.5km/h, did 0-100km in 16.8 seconds, and consumed 11.6 liters per 100km for 7925DM. Equivalent test figures for the Opel Rekord 1700S with 75bhp were 152km/h, 16.4 seconds, and 12.4 liters per 100km for 7737DM.

The Opel was a well made, durable sedan, and very popular throughout Europe; upscale examples were sold in the UK. The Renault 16 was also very popular, but longevity and corrosion counted against French and Italian cars, especially Italian cars of the 1960s and 1970s. The fast 1600s on test were the Fiat 125 and New Class BMW 1600. They had respective readouts of 90bhp, 162km/h, 13.1 seconds, 12.8 liters per 100km, 7492DM, and 85bhp, 164km/h, 12.4 seconds, 12.4 liters per 100km, at 8757DM. Yes, the Fiat did more for less, but also it was made by 'Fix It Again Tony'! The BMW showed the trend of people willing to pay around 15% more for prestige mixed with quality.

The VW 411 had substance, but it didn't have the badge, and VW still doesn't. In the late '60s it was hoped

North American Type 4 Variants and four-door sedans came with VW's 003 automatic as standard equipment. (Courtesy Martin Serrano)

NSU did, with the Ro80. The Ro80 in the comparison was the odd car out, in more ways than one. It was a semi-automatic sedan, capable of 180.5km/h, 0-100km/h in 11.9 seconds, with a dual rotor 115bhp motor that guzzled 15.1 liters per 100km, or 17-18mpg. At 14,150DM the Ro80 had a big price tag, and was obviously expensive to feed. Still, the fuel crisis hadn't happened yet. If the new NSU was reliable, like the VW Type 4 proved to be, the Ro80 might have been worth it. However, all that glitters isn't gold. For the NSU's price, a loaded, fuel-injected BMW 2000tii was a much better bet. However, very soon a more sophisticated fuel-injection system could be had on the VW 411.

TEST THE CAR, NOT THE CONCEPT

It is true that the 68bhp carb 411 had slightly bettered its factory figures of 145km/h and 0-100km/h in 18 seconds, on the *Autotest* run. However,

greater gains were on the way, with the fuel-injected VW 411E. This model's computer controlled injection offered something for 1970 that rivals couldn't. The 411E ushered in the first 100mph production Volkswagen, although factory figures suggested 96mph and 0-62mph in 17 seconds with a four-speed. Britain's *Motor* magazine, in its Road Test No 14/70, found the 411LE four-door capable of more than that.

Indeed, *Motor* discovered that if one was willing to look beyond the anti air-cooled hype, and front-wheel drive obsessiveness, a very decent near luxury sedan would be found in VW's new 411E/LE. The journal titled its injected 411 report "Much Improved 411," and stated "Fuel-injection gives competitive performance; roomy and comfortable, but poor driving position; engine noisy, good road holding; well finished." Objectively investigated, the 411E/LE brought VW vices and benefits that were expected, but some surprisingly good qualities.

A 1972 North American spec 411 Variant, in Turquoise Metallic. At 178.1in long, the 411 Variant was slightly shorter than its sedan counterpart. (Courtesy Martin Serrano)

1972 was the North American Type 4's first full model year. The full Euro 80bhp from the 1700 D-jet flat-four was available, even in California. With a 400-liter 'frunk,' the Type 4 was commodious; the wagon Variant even more so. (Courtesy Martin Serrano)

There had never been a production VW with such a fine turn of speed, and in countries like Britain, Canada and West Germany, a four-speed four-door Type 4 could acquit itself respectably. *Motor*'s mean maximum recorded speed was 100mph (160.9km/h), with an average of 96.7mph, the quarter mile in 19.5 seconds, and 0-60mph in 13.8 seconds. Overall fuel consumption was 23.5mpg (UK), or 12 liters per 100km. The figures placed the 411LE mid pack, when comparing acceleration times of possible Type 4 rivals recently tested by *Motor*.

The 411LE came fourth, behind the Fiat 125 Special, Renault 16TS and Sunbeam Rapier Overdrive. The selected rivals were sports oriented versions. However, the VW placed ahead of the Wolseley 18/85S, Triumph 2000 Overdrive and Citroën DS19 Special. Once again it should be remembered that attempting sustained, flat out cruising in some non German cars, could result in engine damage. British consumer magazine *Which?* managed to get a used Aston Martin DB6 up to 135mph, when the engine showed signs of seizing.

The early '70s was still an era when national car design traits were apparent. It was expected to find a

floaty, soft ride in a French car, and an Italian driving position best enjoyed by the possessor of long arms and short legs. What was unexpected was the Type 4's abundance of interior space, comfort and trunk volume. The very accommodating interior was shown with a lady enjoying the fully reclined front seats. As with many European cars the reclining seat function could be utilized to make a full bed, just like the Ramblers of yesteryear. There were map pockets on the seatbacks, and rear legroom was judged adequate.

Ergonomically there was the problem of having to sit too close to the steering wheel to fully disengage the clutch. It helped to be long of limb, but of course, in America, Type 4 four-doors came with automatic transmission standard, Variants too. *Motor* said the 411LE rode well, and was well insulated from rough surfaces that usually cause rattles in a unibody. Tires specified in this market were Michelin ZX 155SR rubber, on 4.5in wide steel rims, radials naturally.

Such unusual plushness from Wolfsburg elicited the comment from *Motor* that since the Type 3 1500, VW had attempted to diversify its range. They added that the new

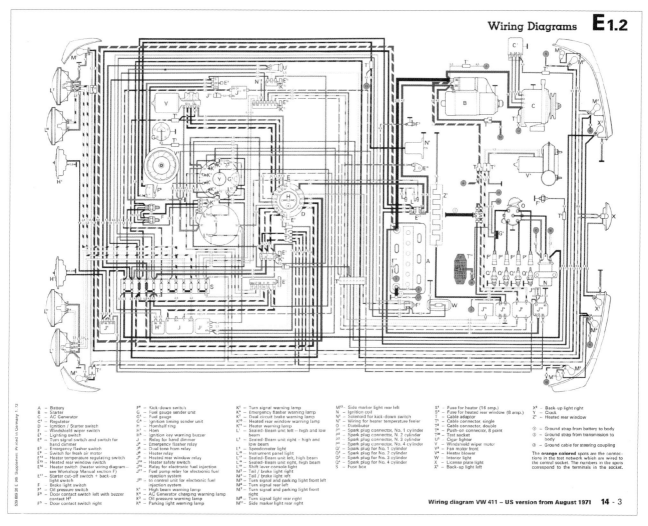

Wiring Diagrams E1.2

Wiring diagram VW 411 – US version from August 1971 14 - 3

411 was designed for a higher price sector than that previously inhabited by VW. Back in 1960 the Big Three US automakers muscled into VW's economy car territory with the Corvair, Falcon and Valiant. A decade later and VW was taking on the Big Three, on the Continent and in Britain too. More precisely, the Big Three's overseas subsidiaries. In Britain this was formerly the Ford Consul, Zephyr class and Vauxhall Victor domain.

In the T4's era there was the Ford UK Corsair and soon to arrive Ford Cortina Mk III. Ford Europe would also do the 17M/20M to replace the 1972 Consul/Granada. Such Dagenham

delights could be up-trimmed and option packed to the eyeballs, in Dearborn tradition. However, such British built Fords lacked one option that was standard at Wolfsburg ... quality. The same could be said of GM's operation named Vauxhall. British designed and made family sedans with trans-Atlantic personality, that were basically two tone and tailfins in the '50s, and Coke bottle styling in the '60s.

The British Vauxhalls shared the Coke bottle look with contemporary Fords. However, even these Vauxhalls struggled to match the quality and rust resistance of Dagenham. Squarely in

This is the wiring diagram for the '72 MY US spec VW 411. All American 411s were injected to beat smog. (Courtesy Volkswagen AG)

97

The low profile Type 3 and Type 4 flat fours made Variant wagons possible. VW's new semi-trailing arm rear suspension helped, too. (Courtesy Martin Serrano)

(Opposite) With automatic transmission and a roomy backseat, the Type 4 was a limousine compared to Beetles sold in '50s America. (Courtesy Martin Serrano)

the VW 411's domain was the Luton built FD Victor, a four-door sedan or wagon, with unitary construction and 1.6/2.0-liter single overhead cam inline fours. A good match for the 411, and produced between 1967 and 1972 with nearly 200,000 made. An attractive, fine-handling conventional family car, but poorly assembled and quick to corrode. Beauty was skin deep, but easy to advertise. The VW's mainstream rivals had the form, but not the 411's substance.

For a really British car in the 411's class, there was the Austin 1800 or Landcrab. Between 1968 and 1975 around 100,000 were made during the British Leyland era. Instead of putting all the hardware at the rear, like the 411, the Landcrab used a transverse engine and front-drive to achieve its interior space. With the Issigonis adherence to functional space efficiency, it compromised on looks – perhaps more so than the Type

4. More crucially relative to the 411, the Austin 1800 Mk II and Mk III didn't offer Wolfsburg quality or reliability.

The 411 didn't have to look for rivals. There was the very strong selling Peugeot 504, Saab 99 and Volvo 144. If the NHTSA's 35mph crash test was anything to go by, the 504 was best avoided. All were in the Type 4's era and price range. Once again, unlike small cars having to challenge the Beetle, here VW was trying to convince Ford, Volvo, Renault, and other buyers to take a chance on the 411. If they had, then like *Motor* magazine they might have discovered how much VW handling had improved with the Type 4. *Motor* experienced little body roll, and final oversteer was only an issue on greasy surfaces. The old Beetle bugbear of swing axle suspension-induced rear wheel tuck in and wild oversteer were absent.

On the negative side, *Motor* found

the 411LE's non power recirculating ball steering a little less responsive than with an earlier test of the carb 411. Other problems were a windshield wiper pattern still set for left-hand drive, and a gasoline heater (Eberspacher) only useable if the Type 4 was stationary. The wiper pattern was a common failing of Continental cars. Porsche kept the LHD wiper pattern going for the 924 and 944 throughout the 1980s.

Motor considered the 411's fashionable front overhang as helping with VW's newly found trunk space. In addition, C pillar vents aided stale air extraction. So, the 411LE had many objective benefits, including now standard dual headlights in the UK. However, was being sensible still enough in 1970? On the practicality front, the new Ford Mk III Cortina had an attractive wagon with four doors. It was more pressure on the VW Variant, from the World's second biggest automaker.

If there was one place the Type 4 should have been, it was North America. This market had been a VW stronghold for 20 years. Now, finally, VW had a suitably sized, compact size rated machine for the USA. A genuine, fully automatic gearbox, and pollution taming electronic fuel-injection from 1970. It all made the 411 seem kinda relevant, and yet ... It seemed with all the attention given to getting the high volume Super Beetle ready for '71 MY, and resources towards the hot selling Audi 100, that the VW 411 was placed on the back burner.

In America the Type 4, as the 411, got a very late 1971 model year release. It arrived in April 1971, and the model year ends in July. A disorganized state of affairs, given VW had been in synch with the American model year since 1955, under Heinz Nordhoff's instigation. The lack of planning was revealed by the 1971 US brochure. Only the VW 411 four-door and Variant were in evidence. The 411 two-door was around, but not shown in the brochure. In America the injection 'E' suffix was omitted. It was superfluous, given all American Type 4s would be fuel-injected.

Perhaps VW got it wrong by dropping that 'E'? Mercedes and Volvo carried the 'E' suffix, in all markets for the fuel-injected versions. In German injection starts with 'E,' and Mercedes, Volvo and VW all used the same German Bosch system. Given the Bosch D-jet setup was much discussed in VW 411/412 ads, VW should have kept the 'E' for image. It would have alerted buyers to injection being inside, like Intel did later with their Pentium processor. American 411/412s also did without the 'L' suffix, since all US Type 4s were in luxury spec anyway. It was possible to buy a 411/412 four-

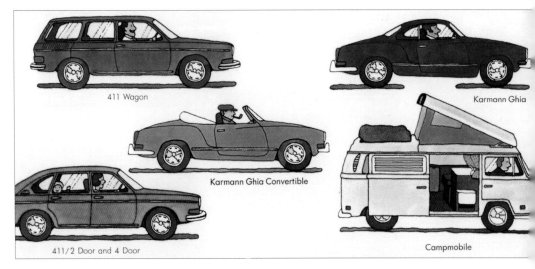

In VW's 1971 range it was still an all air-cooled world. Even the K70 wasn't shown! (Courtesy Volkswagen AG & Ton Ketelaars)

411 Wagon

Karmann Ghia

Karmann Ghia Convertible

411/2 Door and 4 Door

Campmobile

speed in Canada, however in America this was only possible on two-door Fastbacks.

VWoA reasoned that the two-door sedan's sportier nature warranted four on the floor, whereas the more family directed four-door and Variant came standard with VW's fully automatic three-speeder. *Road & Track* gave the 411 a fair hearing, by electing to test the car, rather than debate the issue of whether air-cooled, rear-engined cars were relevant to modern 1970s motoring. Its February 1971 issue carried a full test of the 1971 411 four-door automatic. Echoing Henry Manney's positive earlier comments, concerning the 411 Coupe and Variant, *R&T* noted that on the pre US release test drive the 411 had been well received by the viewing public.

On American streets the 411 proved a positive attention getter, and the volks knew it was a VW. *R&T* felt the long hood look was reminiscent of the Renault 16. The journal speculated that the 411's slow European sales were due to public resistance to the concept of a 'pricey' VW. Indeed, the magazine found the 411 to be somewhat of a diamond in the Wolfsburg rough, as it were.

General noise levels were found to be lower than in other VWs. Plus, the 411 was judged less susceptible to sidewinds than even the revised '71 Super Beetle. This was even though said 1302 Bug shared its general suspension layout with the Type 4.

The 411's longer than Beetle/T3 98.4in wheelbase, and more even

VW got industrial designer Brooks Stevens to makeover the Type 4 into the 412. Stevens also designed the Excalibur that Hidemi Aoki is posing with. (Courtesy www.nepoeht.com)

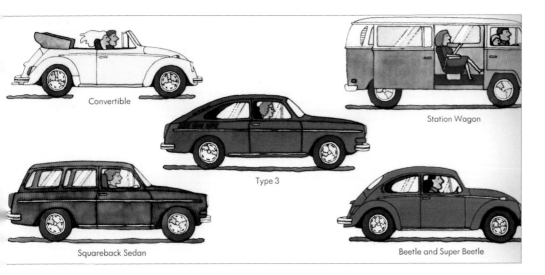

Convertible

Station Wagon

Type 3

Squareback Sedan

Beetle and Super Beetle

weight distribution, were a boon to roadability. The VW 411 could be driven with some spirit, but it wasn't a sports car. Sporty natured cars of the day were around the 0.7g mark on the skidpad, and *R&T*'s 411 four-door managed 0.609g. Given the 155-15 tires on 15 x 4.5in rims, the results were par for the course, and in line with the results of contemporary Mercedes and Volvo sedans.

The journal found power steering to be unnecessary, but had reservations concerning suspension settings. Front springing was stiff, and ride height

high, to compensate for a full luggage load. In contrast the rear suspension adopted a tail down stance, with soft springs for low rear-end roll stiffness. It all created a slightly odd looking high front end, propensity to tail bottoming on rough surfaces, and longitudinal pitching on undulating roads. Enthusiasts have played around with suspension settings to ease these concerns.

In spite of the aforementioned negative points, the 411 proved a good handling family car, with less pitfalls than a Beetle. It took a lot more

VW Brasil made the Type 1-based Brasilia/Variant II from 1973-82. The Brasilia sold over one million units, and utilized a hatchback body. It looked not unlike a 412 Variant. (Courtesy Vereinigte Motor-Verlage)

This European spec 412 was delivered on July 28 1973. Whereas America continued with fuel-injection for '74 MY, Europe went back to dual carbs. (Courtesy Julien Faude)

pushing before it would reveal its rear engine location. The combination of stout Beetlesque structure, albeit in unibody form, with soft European-style suspension settings, produced a comfy riding machine when road surfaces were imperfect. Comfort was aided by good interior space, and front seats on a curved track. A rocking adjuster tilted the whole seat. No stock Bug ever came with a fold-down rear armrest!

Thoughtful touches included having a headlight switch that cancelled when the ignition was turned off, which was handy – no more flat batteries from accidentally leaving on the lights overnight! The six window sedan afforded good outward visibility, and the presence of a B pillar boosted passive safety in an era when hardtops still ruled the fashion stakes. The automatic had been set up to take the motor to the 5200rpm redline in first and second, when flooring the gas pedal, so there was no performance advantage to be gained via manual shifting.

The VW's automatic was a *real* automatic, and the choke was, too, because this car had fuel-injection. The 411 was set up for 'no muss, no fuss' family car driving. No, it

wouldn't cut a fine dash like the latest pony car, or European sports car. Even its quasi stablemate, the VW/Porsche 914, led in the style stakes. However, the 24/24 warranty and *R&T*'s proven 297-mile cruising range was attractively practical. So, too, the four free electronic inspections. Computer diagnosis connector analysis was available at one of many nationwide VW dealerships.

Road & Track found its test 411 sedan to be very well made, and with first class materials. Paint and interior/exterior trim were excellent, but, in true German tradition, the interior was very plain. Still, compared to the Russian roulette lottery of quality usually found on a domestic car, the 411 was in a league of its own. Many buyers in the upscale midsize sedan class were considering an imported car, instead of the usual Oldsmobile, Mercury, etc, standbys. Smaller size for the little lady, and great handling and better gas mileage were reasons for the transition, accelerated after the fuel crisis. However, there were still sound reasons to stay with home-grown.

American-made near luxury midsizers were often more durable concerning power trains, corrosion-resistant bodies and suspension hardware. Good air-conditioning systems and decent performance with an automatic transmission were also a given. These were practical questions the 1971 VW 411 could answer better than the fancy pants Audi 100LS. Good performance with an automatic box, the 411 did this better than the glacial Volvo 144. VW's confidence in this arena was displayed by most American spec 411/412s having automatic as standard. Many imports stuck with a stick.

VW was still offering the most comprehensive and longest warranty in the business. They did this slightly earlier than American Motors with its soon famous Buyer Protection Plan. Even compared to this, VW offered 24/24 as standard on 411, Beetle, Thing, and indeed all its air-cooled vehicles. It should be remembered that VW had the largest dealer network in America, out of the imported brands. It was something VWoA had been

building on since the '50s. The network went with an excellent parts supply back up, and dealer mechanics that knew air-cooled VWs.

You probably wouldn't find a Renault or Fiat dealer in the Midwest, but you most likely would locate a VW sales and service outlet. The 411 was good on paper and in reality, combining durability and practicality. Not to mention quality that even a 1971 Caddy would like to have. However, were people feeling the good vibes, and keeping an open mind concerning air-cooled VWs? *R&T* said the 411 had much to offer: a roomy family car, that was well made, and worked well with automatic transmission. However, the journal did say it preferred the front engine/front-drive route to efficient transport in a moderately sized family car. In the early '70s, opinion and choice seemed governed more by ideology than reality.

The 411's quasi stablemate the Audi 100, seemed to represent the near

When testing the new VW 412 in 1973, Car and Track's Bud Lindemann noted the 412's bigger taillights, versus the 411. The new squared-off lens shape served as a side marker function. (Courtesy Hilmar Walde)

VWoA ads still played on the old VW touchstones in 1973: VWs were affordable and reliable. Come the '75 MY Rabbit, and both qualities were in question. (Courtesy Volkswagen AG)

A$3299*Volkswagen?

Yep.
That's the price.
And that's the Volkswagen.
The 1973 Volkswagen 412 Wagon.
If you think that's shocking, wait till you see what you get for the money.
First, there's a magnesium alloy engine, run by a computerized system no domestic car has:
Electronic fuel injection.
It gives you quick starts, smooth acceleration.
Then, too, the 412 has the world's only

timed preheating system.
Which warms up its plush interior, without you running the engine. Or even sitting in the car.
What's more, we think if you're going to pay more for a Volkswagen, you're entitled to get more great features, also as standard equipment.
Like steel-belted radial tires. Metallic paint. Front disc brakes. Rear-window defogger. Automatic transmission. Plenty of luggage space in back. And a big trunk in front.

And more. Lots more.
Fact is, the 412 is so well engineered, it has the world's longest full-car warranty. (Excluding only Rolls-Royce.)
24 months/24,000 miles.*
So what's really shocking isn't that we ask $3299 for a Volkswagen that gives you so much.
But that other carmakers ask $3299 for a car that doesn't give you so much.

Introducing the 1973 Volkswagen 412
Few things in life work as well as a Volkswagen

*Volkswagen of America, Inc. *1973 Volkswagen 412 Wagon suggested retail price, P.O.E. Local taxes and other dealer charges, if any, additional. *If an owner maintains and services his vehicle in accordance with the Volkswagen maintenance schedule any factory part found to be defective in material or workmanship within 24 months or 24,000 miles, whichever comes first (except normal wear and tear and service items) will be repaired or replaced by any U.S. or Canadian Volkswagen Dealer. And this will be done free of change. See your dealer for details.*

luxury class, front-drive utopia many wanted, or thought they wanted. Front-drive, it's so modern! Even puritanical *Consumer Reports* was seduced by the Audi 100, noting the interior space afforded comfort, concerning steering wheel clearance – even for portly drivers. Then there was the Middle Pressure carb fed inline four, with its

The buildsheet for this '73 412LE was discovered under the back seat. A rare find, and an archive item from air-cooled Wolfsburg days! (Courtesy Lars Sellbom)

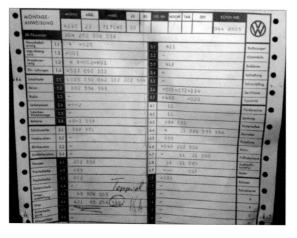

high specific output. However, as the same journal said when testing a W116 Mercedes 280S automatic, teaming a high output motor to an automatic was like hitching a race horse to a plow.

The VW 411 put its money on torque, and unlike the carburettor Audi and Mercedes, had fuel-injection as standard. This was quite an asset, especially considering the one-class-up VW K70 didn't have injection at any price. *Road & Track* found the 411 sedan capable of 84mph at 4700rpm. This top speed was also the car's sustainable cruising speed, and well short of the T4 motor's 5200rpm redline. At 60mph the 411 registered 3330rpm. This maintained the VW tradition of comfortable freeway cruising. The relatively tall for VW 3.67:1 final drive ratio helped bring cruising calmness.

A brake swept area of 311in^2 reduced the panic of panic stops. Indeed, the 2430lb 411 automatic had nearly the same amount of brakes as the new '70 ½ Camaro 350. However, Camaro's 332in^2 had to persuade 3670lb worth of coupe to halt! The VW 411 had 11.1in front disk brakes, 9.8 x 1.78in rear drums, versus Camaro's 11in disks and 9.5 x 2in rear drum stoppers. *R&T* found the Chevy's brakes faded a lot more: to maintain deceleration in six stops from 60mph, pedal effort went up 270% in the Camaro, but only 75% in VW. For mountain road driving, the VW was a safer bet.

The 5.7-liter Camaro took six seconds to accomplish the 50-70mph overtaking maneuver. The VW 411, from 1.7 liters of displacement, took 7.1 seconds. In normal driving *R&T* recorded 14.4mpg in the Chevy, but 22.5mpg in the VW. With its 300 horse SS350 motor, the Camaro cost $4673 with a/c. The VW 411 cost $3109 sans a/c, but you got the benefit of standard radials. VW dock installed a/c went for under $300. Of course, the 411 didn't cut as dashing a figure as the Camaro. However, the VW could carry more people and their luggage in greater comfort. In addition, VW offered double the Chevy warranty.

VW still seemed to do things differently to everyone else. *R&T* found the front disks locked, at a time when many cars locked their rear brakes. The latter accompanied by a good deal of tail slewing. As a luxury economy car concept, the 411 was perhaps five years too early for North America. *Road & Track* said the expected line, about the 411 being the perfect car for VW air-cooled devotees to trade up to. If only it looked like a Mercedes! In the spirit of VW evolution, 1972 411s featured a new four-spoke safety steering wheel, and windshield wiper control was now done via column stalk action. 1971 411s had seen the demise of the three-spoke tiller and the old-fashioned wiper control dashboard knob. However, 1971 dashboards featured a matt black finish, instead of faux woodgrain.

VW SEEKS SAFETY

It was wise of VW to improve interior safety. After all, lobby groups were pushing for increases in auto safety, and reductions in auto pollution. The same year as the 1970 Muskie Smog Bill, came the federal government's ESV (Experimental Safety Vehicle) initiative. Companies under contract would create vehicles that weighed 4000lb and meet proposed 1974 smog law, that could pass certain safety tests. The idea was to see how much safety could be built into a modern car, and from this what future laws concerning auto safety should be.

US corporations Fairchild, AMF and

A pregnant ladybird (Super Beetle) and loaf of bread (Variant), but no Archie Bunker! 1973 was the final year for an all air-cooled lineup. (Courtesy Volkswagen AG)

The $3300 1973 412 did indeed have the suspension layout of a sports car. The MacPherson struts and semi-trailing arms were held in common with the Porsche 914 and 911. (Courtesy Volkswagen AG)

The Type 4 had solid, practical features, but lacked the svelte, easy sell styling of fellow near-luxury class Audi 100. It was easier bait which helped Ingolstadt connect with buyers. (Courtesy Volkswagen AG)

Have two doors kept you out of a Volkswagen?

Don't answer yet.
The car in the picture is a Volkswagen.
And, as you can see, it has four doors.
It's our new 411 4-Door sedan.
Like most 4-door sedans, our 411 gives the people in the back almost as much room as the people in the front.

Unlike most 4-door sedans, though, there's also room for luggage in the front as well as in back.
Like most 4-door sedans, our 411 has an engine.
Unlike most 4-door sedans, our engine gets about 22 miles to the gallon.
Like most 4-door sedans, our 411 offers a lot of options. Auto-

matic transmission, radial tires, rear-window defogger, to name a few.
Unlike most 4-door sedans, those options are included in the price of the car.
Now you can answer if you like.
[ ] Yes.
[ ] No.

With all those interfamilial VW Group rivals the 412 was facing, it was hard to see the Type 4's woodgrain for the trees! (Courtesy David Hill)

GM were under contract, but Mercedes, BMW, Volvo, VW and others were working on safety cars of their own. VW's boss of their safety program in 1972 was Dr Ernst Fiala, and VW had come up with a more modestly sized safety car of 110in wheelbase, 186in length and under 3000lb. The four-door car had the basic silhouette of the upcoming Passat, and a front fascia not unlike the pending VW 412. Like other automakers, VW wasn't too enamored with airbags as a passive restraint system. It preferred an automatic vacuum belt system.

Although receiving no funds from the American government, VW was working in cooperation with the DOT (Department of Transportation) concerning its ESV's development.

Wolfsburg had different layouts for the prototypes it built. The first two had rear air-cooled 1.8-liter units. The third had a front-drive, transverse engine layout, with a VW designed engine dating back to late 1969. The powerplant was not Audi/NSU related.

The ideas from VW's ESV were applicable to the VW Type 4 and the Audi 100. VW's ESV program had started in 1969. The rear-engined nature of the first two protos shows that under Dr Kurt Lotz VW hadn't abandoned rear-engined mainstream vehicles at this stage. However, the front-drive format of its third ESV was indicative of the direction the company would take.

Actions do indeed speak louder than words, because under then current leader, Rudolf Leiding, VW's chief engineer and ex Mercedes man Ludwig Kraus was developing a kit car system. This new plan would bring VW into line with its European rivals. It was Leiding that steered the corporation towards front-drive. The new beginning was the Passat clone of the 1972 Audi 80. Now VW would have a new generation of front-drive machines, that were highly hardware interrelated. The motivation for the change, apart from trying to find a future range of high volume selling VWs, was the loss of the economy car market to the Japanese automakers.

As of late 1972, VW was now the fourth largest car manufacturer in the World. Wolfsburg had been overtaken by Toyota, so that the global Big Three were now GM first, Ford second and Toyota third. Changing fortunes had been swift since the late '60s. In 1955, VW was America's top imported brand, selling 28,097 units that year. In October 1972, *CAR*'s Marc Madow took a look at the Subaru Leone. He felt the Leone to be a competitive threat to Fiat's 128, a car of similar front-drive layout. Fortunately the

A UK market 1973 VW 412LS. Only top line spec UK 'LS' editions were around, and that implied the sporty D-jet injected Type 4 1700. (Courtesy David Hill)

European Economic Community (EEC) had a big trade protection wall to keep European manufacturers safe from those well made, reliable Datsuns and Toyotas!

America had a more open door policy to trade, and this gave Japanese companies a chance, just like with VW back in the 1950s. In 1972, Subaru hoped to sell 25,000 cars in America. Toyota sold that number in 1965, and by 1972 it had overtaken American Motors and was putting the wasabi heat on Volkswagen.[10] The reasons were obvious, the Japanese offered a dependable, well assembled small car, at a low price. They also had a growing network of good sales and service agents. It was all just like VW had done earlier, but Toyotas and Datsuns were modern looking, and came with lots of standard comfort and convenience equipment.

VW was seeking new models for passive and sales safety. In the short run, and before the new Passat could arrive Stateside, Wolfsburg gave the Type 4 a makeover. For 1973 model year the VW 411 was no more … say hello to the 412! Engineering-wise the 411 and 412 were very much alike. The 80 horse electronic D-jet 1700 carried over, so too the policy of standard automatic transmission for four-door sedans and two-door Variants, not forgetting the 411's MacPherson strut front suspension and rear semi-trailing arm set up.

BROOKS STEVENS & THE 412

The Eberspacher was still pre-warming your interior in the Ozarks too. However, now the Type 4 had a new name and a new look. The person VW got to restyle the Type 4 was legendary American industrial designer Brooks Stevens. If you have ever admired the restrooms of the Milwaukee Railroad Company's trains, thank Mr Brooks Stevens. Stevens was innovative in

That the VW Type 4 was more attractive than the BMC/BL 'Landcrab' was up for debate. However, the VW's greater reliability and quality were proven. (Courtesy David Hill)

The coast was clear for the 412 in 1973. However, the following model year saw the new Passat eat into 412 sales, as buyers looked to downsize in the post fuel crisis recession. The Type 4 was the first VW to reach 100mph in independent testing. The 1974 412LS tied with the Passat 1500 on top speed, but beat it for interior space and ride comfort. (Courtesy David Hill)

the use of Formica. More than that, he designed the Hiawatha express trains, that all the stuff went into! Further Milwaukee connection, in that Brooks Stevens also designed Harley Davidson motorcycles.

The Milwaukee-born designer was probably the ideal person to redo VW's Type 4. Stevens popularized the term planned obsolescence. He described the concept as creating the desire in the consumer for something better, and sooner. Although VW seemed the polar opposite to the Big Three style of 'nothing older than last year's car model,' there was some similarity between Stevens' thinking and Beetle evolution. That is, all those annual incremental changes, features and improvements did make buyers want the latest version of Wolfsburg's work.

Adolf Hitler ordered the creation of The People's Car. However, high level Nazis, if archive footage and episodes of *Hogan's Heroes* are anything to go by, liked to ride around in Mercedes. Brooks Stevens' Excalibur tribute to vintage motoring was inspired by the 1928 Mercedes SSK. Stevens also had a famous association with Studebaker, having redesigned the 1962 Studebaker Gran Turismo Hawk. The firm's Avanti sports car was well known for its grilleless front and countersunk headlamps, not unlike the original VW Type 4. Although Brooks Stevens didn't do the Avanti (that had been overseen by designer Raymond Loewy), the 412 was a chance to create another auto extrovert.

Perhaps there is no better qualification for reworking the Type 4 than having designed the Oscar Mayer Wienermobile. What could be more German than a mobile mini frank on four wheels! So it was that VW financed new front fenders, hood and front fascia for the 1973-74 Type 4. The newly-named Type 4 412 had grown a little: the sedan was now 180.4in, and the Variant 179.3in. Front and rear tracks were marginally different at 54.6in and 53in respectively. Weight between the 411 and pre impact bumper 412 remained equal; so, too, the 64.4in width and 58.5in height.

The altered look of the 412, echoed the style of cars made by VW do Brasil. The T1-based VW Brasilia and Brazilian Type 3s have a VW family resemblance: however would car buyers ever warm to this general styling? In the UK it seemed consumers liked Italian designed cars that resembled hatchbacks and had flat sides. The Pininfarina-styled Austin 1100/1300, and later VW Golf by Giugiaro, are examples. It seems many put up with the so-called 'Ugly Bug' for decades, since it didn't break down. Soon, the fashionistas would have water-cooled icons of front-drive style. However, first there was the 1973 412 to evaluate.

VW 412 VERSUS VW PASSAT – CAR AND TRACK

It isn't often you get to compare two cars under the same conditions, on the same track, and driven by the same test driver. However, this very opportunity was afforded by the TV show *Car and Track* in 1973-74, hosted by Bud Lindemann. This nationally syndicated show had a car test segment. Reflecting the nature of the North American car market before the mid '70s, the vast majority of test subjects were domestic. Of the few imports looked at, VWs figured prominently. Indeed, for many years the words import and VW were synonymous.

After evaluating cars at Waterford Hills Raceway during 1972, *Car and*

Track reverted to its Grand Rapids Michigan Grattan Raceway test track in 1973. It was here on Michigan plates that a 1973 Turquoise Metallic 412 four-door, dubbed by Lindemann as a berlina beauty, was put through its paces by *Car and Track*'s resident hotshoe. In keeping with American Type 4s it was an automatic, which was standard equipment. Being a 49 state car, this 412 still sported the familiar 80-horse 'hi po' 1700 Bosch D-jet injected motor.

At nearly one gross horsepower per cube, 102.5ci, the OHV flat-four would certainly have been considered high output in the '60s. For a stock standard air-cooled Vee Dub motor, it was uncommonly lively. Sadly, if one was under the grip of Governor Reagan in the Golden State, the 412's 1700 only made 72bhp, such was the price of

clean air in that locality. Whereas 49 state Type 4s retained their 8.2:1 CR, 1973 Californian 412s were down to 7.3:1. Who says it never rains in sunny California?

First off, Bud Lindemann remarked on how the Type 4's restyling job ran to new front fenders, hood and bigger taillights. Then came performance testing, and the admission that all 2500lb came out of the hole in pretty good shape. Zero to thirty in 4.4 seconds, 0-45mph in 6.7 seconds, and 0-60mph in 11.3 seconds. Before the auto industry became engulfed in downsizing post-World Fuel Crisis No 1, the VW 412 was rated as a compact. Lindemann noted they achieved 20mpg on test, which covered a wide variety of usage: city driving, highway running, and not forgetting the exuberant, gay abandon with which

When testing the Type 4 in its November 14 1968 issue, Autocar said, "The car has that 'unbreakable' feeling of all VWs, and both corners and rides very well indeed." A 1973 Variant automatic is shown here. (Courtesy Jeremiah Berger)

To activate the Eberspacher (gasoline heater), fully pull up the lever right of the handbrake. The dashboard's green lamp and cooling system fan will both come on. Pull up the lever left of the handbrake and the gas pump and Eberspacher will operate until the engine makes enough heat.

Below: This is the later four-vent 412 underdash evaporator/blower a/c assembly from DPD. (Courtesy Jeremiah Berger)

Car and Track's test driver flung all test subjects around the racetrack.

That kind of acceleration, with economy, from an automatic 1.7-liter four banger showed tremendous efficiency for the day. By way of comparison, the 6.6-liter AMC Matador X 401 coupe was tested by *Car and Track* in 1974, and achieved 0-60mph in 11.6 seconds, plus 11.3mpg. The Matador X's 401 4 bbl V8 was rated at the same 255 horses during 1972-74. The VW 412's figures showed future expectations in automotive design.

There was demand for more performance from smaller engines, and greater accommodation and luggage capacity from smaller bodies. A small car that felt like a big car, and the 412 was an incremental step towards that goal. In fact, with downsizing from the fuel crisis on the horizon, the compact of the '70s, became the midsize car of the '80s. The 412's disk/drum brakes were generously sized. They were in keeping with what you would find on a 3500lb domestic intermediate. So, it came as little surprise that VW's compact did well in *Car and Track*'s braking test: from 30mph the 412 shut down in 39ft, from 50mph in 93ft and from 70mph in 197ft.

More important than the braking numbers was the Type 4's behavior during the test. Stops were straight and true, and with minimal fade, even after eight stops to heat up the brakes around the test track. The Beetle was also famous for minimal brake fade. It all made VW your amigo in times of need, especially when it came to mountain road driving. Indeed, compared to domestic cars, whose brake pedal faded nearly to the floor, accompanied by tail slewing brought about by locked rear binders, the VW seemed more secure. In handling slalom tests the Beetle and 412 that *Car and Track* tested both behaved like sportscars compared to many domestic midsize and full-size lead sleds.

In contrast to domestic cars where power steering was lost from an inability of the pump to keep up with frequent and sharp changes in direction, air-cooled VWs displayed fast, accurate steering. Good tracking and recovery through the cones were in evidence. The Super Beetle and 412's semi-trailing arm rear suspension also didn't exhibit jacking up, as

momentum built up when exiting the final cone. Bud Lindemann did note however, that the 412's responsive steering and slalom prowess weren't carried through to general track driving.

During track action the 412 four-door's front end stuck well, but the rear felt light. The motor lacked the muscle to induce power oversteer when the front end washed out, or lapsed into understeer. Grattan Raceway had a very tricky section – a high speed, reverse camber turn. On this part of the course the 412's rear end came around as the front wheels came off the deck. It was like axle tramp in reverse, as the test driver temporarily lost steering control. In contrast, in 1973 *Car and Track* tried two sporty cars that did well on the reverse camber section.

The Century-based Buick Grand Sport 455 Stage One was a supercar version of the steed Kojak trusted on TV. It took the reverse camber turn at 75mph, staying flat and in control. The same was the case with a '73

The Type 4's 98.4in wheelbase afforded a spacious rear compartment by VW standards. A 1973 TV commercial billed the 412 as VW's luxury car. See www.youtube.com/watch?v=GMyJ8GM1ip0. (Courtesy Jeremiah Berger)

Wolfsburg's first four-door design was the Type 4; its second was the Passat. (Courtesy Lars Sellbom)

Plymouth 'Cuda 340. Both cars took the turn flat, and in a four wheel drift. Of course, both were conventional front-engined cars, with heavy-duty suspension and wide section bias belted rubber. It was crucial that rear-engined cars had their tire pressures adjusted, as per manufacturer specification.

Oftentimes cars were delivered to magazines in the '60s and '70s, with incorrectly set tire pressures, along with many other assembly line maladies. This was the case with *Road & Track*'s December 1968 issue VW 1600 Squareback. Before re-adjusting tire pressures back to the correct levels, the magazine described the Squareback's handling as "thoroughly spooky." *Car and Track* had a policy of testing cars exactly as delivered. A case in point was their evaluation of a '69 Impala 396 sedan. Here, the left front tire was so

under-inflated, it nearly came off the rim during track cornering. This might have been related to why the brakes were pulling to the left so severely. So much so, that said Impala performed an unintentional reverse J turn during panic stop braking!

In other aspects of handling, *Car and Track*'s 412 seemed to perform satisfactorily. Although it should also be noted, that *Car and Track*'s 1974 Super Beetle didn't loose composure on the reverse camber portion of the test track. This might suggest the 412 wasn't set up properly. Then again, it might also just mean that the less powerful Bug was carrying less speed through the turn, so oversteer didn't manifest itself. Lindemann did say *Car and Track* tended to run the slalom cones a little slower in VW Beetles. He believed lowering the center of gravity through reduced ride height would reduce chances of wild oversteer and make the cars safer.

Judging matters overall, the rear-engined VWs were shown by *Car and Track* to have excellent traction off the line. The Super Beetle's mountain master first gear made for the Bug's usual jack rabbit start. The same applied to the 412. However, in this case, off the line alacrity was due to a torque rich, injected flat-four with tuned intake runners, and the torque amplifying effects of a conventional torque converter automatic. Bud Lindemann mentioned that the test driver used a 2500rpm brake torqued take off technique to produce the 412's sound acceleration times. This in turn spoke of the 412's good brakes, that they were able to hold the sedan at rest with that many revs on the tach.

Compared to most family type domestics, the traditional VWs moved sharply most of the time. There was that quick manual steering, though perhaps not so quick in the Type 4, due to engineers wanting that huge frunk. It seemed VW wasn't alone in the move to practicality: the Volvo Amazon had been a lively, agile European sedan, like a poor man's Mk II Jag, however, with its new 1967 144, Volvo changed to a heavier, vaguer steering, in the search for a small turning circle. VW wanted a small turning circle too, and got it in the move from Beetle to Super Beetle. Moving into the '70s, family cars were becoming more family car like. Even pony cars were fast being tamed.

The late '60s to early '70s saw much experimentation and debate over the best form of hardware and general layout. Many felt independent suspension was still an unperfected technology, hence the adherence to live axles by the aforementioned Gran Sport and 'Cuda. Their predictable

At -30.4°C in Sweden, the Eberspacher gasoline heater is your friend! (Courtesy Lars Sellbom)

handling lent credence to sticking with tradition, not to mention the cost savings. Alfa Romeo used a well located live axle tethered by links on the '60s Giulia. It then went DeDion with the Alfetta – this was a sort of modified live axle, with flexible joint. Euro cars like the Fiat 131, Rover SD1 3500 and Volvo 740 all used live axles.

The VW Type 4's semi-trailing arm rear suspension proved a marked improvement over the previous swing axle, in terms of reducing camber angle variation and creating secure handling. Daimler-Benz made the same tech transition, for the same reasons. However, like BMW and Porsche 911 too, even semi-trailing arm rear suspension was prone to sudden oversteer at the limit. There was a similar lack of consensus concerning chassis layout. Domestic brands, and their customers, believed

This 1973 412LE four-door has aftermarket Sprintstar rims from famous VW specialist Empi. (Courtesy Lars Sellbom)

for refinement saw Ford switch back to insulated frame construction, with their 1972 midsize line. The VW 412 employed unitary construction, but *Car and Track*'s experience showed an interior ambiance of sound refinement.

There was also debate on engine format. How many cylinders did one need, inline or vee, and what of rotary? Overhead cam or overhead valves? Many engineers considered OHC unnecessary, with engines over 3 liters (180ci). Cost considerations dictated which cars would get fuel-injection, or stay with carbs. Then too, there was the increasing divide between rear-drive lovers and front-drive modernists. A case for the future could be made for light alloy engines, fuel-injection and rear-wheel drive. Ditto concerning the use of overhead valve engines, if the Chevy LS V8 family is anything to go by. The VW Type 4 had all this stuff, but for many the rear engine location was a deal breaker.

Coming into the '70s, the only other internationally available rear-engined cars came from Porsche. Due to reasons of space efficiency hatchback formats and handling concerns, it seemed less likely by the day that a high volume, rear-engined automobile would exist by the 1980s. The irony was that only one car could make that claim in the 1980s … the original VW Beetle. However, such achievements weren't helping the 412 in 1973. In performance evaluation, *Car and Track* judged the 412 as average for the compact segment. The flat-four motor lacked sufficient street moxie to power said VW out of early understeer trackside.

VW hadn't been in the North American compact size class prior to the 411/412. It should be remembered that domestic automakers still offered V8 powered compacts throughout the '70s, which puts *Car and Track*'s

body on frame construction was the best to minimize vibration and rattles, from invading the passenger compartment.

Unibody construction was still looked upon with suspicion concerning refinement, and even crash safety. *Car and Track*'s test of the unitary construction AMC Matador Coupe X 401, bore this out. The coupe did trap a lot of rattles, and the review suggested redesigned suspension and more interior insulation. Many thought unibody cars were like a drum, that amplified NVH. The search average performance assessment in perspective. Like those V8s, the 411/412s mostly had automatic transmission, and VW had an autobox better than many European rides. For a first time compact effort, Wolfsburg had done reasonably with their Type 4. Especially given VW's retention of the increasingly oddball, rear air-cooled motor tradition.

In conclusion Bud Lindemann noted that the 412 was a good looking car, with a well done interior which included wood inlay. He said the car's good points, plus VW's reputation for quality, should make it a good seller. He also echoed the popular Type 4 expectation, that VW finally had a machine for Bug owners to aspire and trade up to: "Then too, at least now a Beetle owner has something to graduate to." This proved partially true, the Type 4 did manage reasonable sales volume in North America, taking into account its short three and a bit, model year availability. A number of Beetle owners did trade up to a Type 4 sedan and Variant. However, a new kind of car sort of explained, why the Type 4 didn't do better.

In 1974 *Car and Track* tried out the new VW Dasher. This was a derivation of the successful '73 MY Audi Fox. As Wolfsburg's latest export to North America, and a new age water-cooled front-driver to boot, Bud Lindemann was enthusiastic. Thinking of the Beetle, he made the statement that the new car outhandled, out-mpg'eed and outperformed any previous VW. He also added, "Then too it even looks more like a car." That last observation was obviously aimed at ye olde Bug!

In truth, the Dasher 1500 four-speed was no faster than the 412 automatic *Car and Track* had tested a year earlier. The Dasher lived up to its name, by hitting 30mph from rest in 3.5 seconds.

As part of the 412's upscale raison d'etre, wood-effect dash was complemented here by non-vinyl satin material seats.

VW offered four on the floor, when many economy cars had three on the tree. However, in place of an overdrive, the Type 4 box had a direct top gear. (Courtesy Lars Sellbom)

However, 0-45mph and 0-60mph times were identical to those achieved by the 412; that is, 6.7 and 11.3 seconds respectively. Indeed, there were many aspects of *Car and Track*'s test, that showed VW's next generation of cars were achieving their results, via lighter weight. The alacrity of the Dasher's 0-30mph clocking was nearly equal to a 7-liter Torino Cobra Jet V8 that *Car and Track* had tried on for size in 1971. It reflected the Dasher's lightweight and great traction.

According to Autocar, the 80bhp injected 1700 shown here cut the 0-60mph dash from 16.5 to 13.8 seconds. Carb or injection, the displacement was still 1.7 liters until the end of '73 MY. (Courtesy Lars Sellbom)

The VW Dasher/Rabbit were certainly generating amazing figures through lower weight. A 1971 Super Beetle 1600 wasn't exactly elephant-like at a mere 1970lb. However, consider that the Audi-engined Euro Golf 1500 was only 1720lb. Tractionwise, VW's excellent results for years came via having an engine placed over the driving wheels. Nose-heavy pony cars had their hind hoofs in the air! It was the same tale with Dasher and Rabbit, except all the hardware was at the front. The Dasher benefited via its Audi style north south I4 being far forward.

The same weight-saving benefits were also displayed in braking and fuel economy tests. Bud Lindemann said of the Dasher, "A VW with disk brakes, wowee!" While Stateside Bugs never got front disk brakes, the Type 3 and Type 4s certainly did, and at a much earlier date. That was the trouble with the new VW front-drivers, they stole all the attention, invited comparisons with Beetle, and caused people to overlook or forget the technical refinements of the Type 3 and Type 4. In braking from 30mph, the Dasher stopped 10ft shorter at 21ft, compared to the 412. Its cold and hot 70mph-0 braking were also slightly shorter, at a respective 189ft and 195ft, versus 412.

Fuel economy in the wake of the first gas crunch was so crucial. The Dasher four-speed did 33mpg in all types of driving, compared to the 412 automatic's 20mpg. Lindemann noted that the 75bhp four banger, almost allowed the Dasher to power through the turns. For great acceleration, braking and gas mileage, thank the Dasher's light weight. Weight was trimmed to 2100lb to produce a strong power to weight ratio. However, this introduced problems on the Dasher/Passat, compared to the 2500lb, size up compact that was VW 412. For one, there was a lack of refinement.

The Dasher on test possessed a rough ride. In the words of Bud Lindemann, "The body seemed to lack the strong heavy feeling of solidarity." This sentiment was echoed across the pond. Here, the UK's ITV channel show *Drive In*, tested the 1975 model year VW Golf (Rabbit). Tester Richard Hudson Evans noted that the Golf's ride comfort was poor, in terms of being choppy. This was especially the case at the back. However, fuel economy for the Golf 1100 was stated as 35mpg, with the 1500 edition on 33mpg (UK mpg). It was also mentioned that in the wake of the energy crisis, such fuel economy figures were of key importance.

Volkswagen's strong suit in past years was as a viable small highway car, providing great gas mileage in the process. The VW 412 seemed to embody this tradition, more so than Dasher. It should be remembered that *Car and Track*'s 412 was an automatic, but the Dasher's figures were from a four-speed manual transmission car. Bud Lindemann said the four-speed car accelerated much faster than the Dasher automatic that they sampled. In addition, independent testing of automatic equipped Foxes, Rabbits and Dashers showed fuel economy and acceleration statistics to be discernibly worse than four-speed editions. This explains why magazines focused their testing on manual gearbox versions.

Road & Track's Dasher/Fox owner survey, showed a mere 14% had chosen automatic transmission. Most Type 4s sold in North America, came with an autobox as standard equipment. *Road & Track* noted that the automatic transmission take up rate on Dasher/Fox was low for a family sedan. Although economy and acceleration figures pointed to a front-drive choice, the 412 seemed more competent as an all purpose family car. *Car and Track*'s 50-70mph passing time for the Dasher four-speed was 7.9 seconds, but *Road & Track* got 7.1 seconds out of its 411 automatic. It also seemed the 412's 400lb weight increase over Dasher was put to good use in refinement.

Bud Lindemann said the Dasher's excellent handling was allied to a rough ride that could prove annoying on long highway trips. As a small family car in America, this compromised its practical value. Lindemann said, "If you are getting divorced from the big car class, it's doubtful you will want to marry a Dasher." He then added, that ex full-size car owners were more likely to consider an intermediate than any car in the subcompact class. That was

The Type 4 flat fours had the VW refinements of aluminum engine cases, and a conventional oil filter. (Courtesy Lars Sellbom)

Optional extra carpet trim was specified for this 412LE's frunk. It took a useful 8.1ft³. (Courtesy Lars Sellbom)

the inference, and the Dasher was certainly a subcompact.

A QUESTION OF VALUE

The other consequence of the fuel crisis, aside from higher gas prices and lengthening gas lines, was inflation. The VW Fox, Dasher, Rabbit and Scirocco were pricey small cars, whereas the Beetle had always been inexpensive. Lindemann concluded, "But if you are a little car lover, then this newest VW will consume about $4000 of pay juice in your next payment book." Four grand was one heck of a price for a subcompact, especially in light of the well equipped and made Datsuns and Toyotas.

It seemed that VW had taken a conscious decision not to engage the Japanese automakers, with their new generation of VW economy cars. However, at four grand for the new Dasher, and the soon to arrive Rabbit lineball with the window sticker of a compact sized six-cylinder Ford Granada, were they really economy cars? It seemed like the consumer was paying an awful lot for some aspects of mechanical efficiency, space utilization and handling prowess.

It was difficult to characterize the direction VW was taking in North America. Difficult to describe, but easy to understand. Wolfsburg knew it couldn't compete with the Japanese in delivering a well built car at a certain price point, with a great deal of standard equipment. The rising Deutschmark, West German labor costs and the efficiency of Japanese

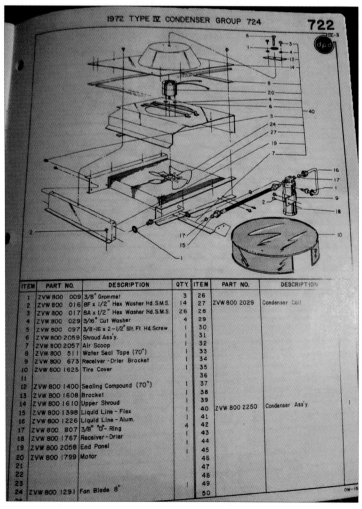

1972 TYPE IV CONDENSER GROUP 724 — 722

ITEM	PART NO.	DESCRIPTION	QTY.	ITEM	PART NO.	DESCRIPTION
1	ZVW 800 009	3/8" Grommet	3	26		
2	ZVW 800 016	8F x 1/2" Hex Washer Hd. S.M.S.	14	27	ZVW 800 2029	Condenser Coil
3	ZVW 800 017	8A x 1/2" Hex Washer Hd. S.M.S.	26	28		
4	ZVW 800 029	3/16" Cut Washer	4	29		
5	ZVW 800 097	3/8-16 x 2-1/2" Slt. Ft. Hd. Screw	1	30		
6	ZVW 800 2059	Shroud Ass'y.	1	31		
7	ZVW 800 2057	Air Scoop	1	32		
8	ZVW 800 511	Water Seal Tape (70")	1	33		
9	ZVW 800 673	Receiver-Drier Bracket	1	34		
10	ZVW 800 1625	Tire Cover	1	35		
11				36		
12	ZVW 800 1400	Sealing Compound (70")	1	37		
13	ZVW 800 1608	Bracket	1	38		
14	ZVW 800 1610	Upper Shroud	1	39		
15	ZVW 800 1398	Liquid Line - Flex	1	40	ZVW 800 2250	Condenser Ass'y.
16	ZVW 800 1226	Liquid Line - Alum.	1	41		
17	ZVW 800 807	3/8" "O"- Ring	4	42		
18	ZVW 800 1767	Receiver-Drier	1	43		
19	ZVW 800 2058	End Panel	1	44		
20	ZVW 800 1799	Motor	1	45		
21				46		
22				47		
23				48		
24	ZVW 800 1291	Fan Blade 8"	1	49		
				50		

If your Type 4 had a/c, you might have found this condenser and fan unit in the spare wheel well. DPD was VWoA's authorized agent for aftermarket a/c. All dealers stocked parts for the system, using a ZVW designation. (Courtesy Volkswagen AG)

VW's Christmas presents for 1973 model year were the new 412, and Beetle 1303! (Courtesy Lars Sellbom)

When it comes to winter traction, rear-engined and front-engined VWs place the motor's weight over the drive wheels. However, the former can hop up the power without torque steer. (Courtesy Lars Sellbom)

assembly plants and their workers, made direct competition impossible. Basically, VW couldn't deliver Beetle quality at a Beetle price, along with all the comfort and gadgets included on Colts, Datsuns and Toyotas.

The result for VWoA was the expensive economy car. However, the concept of spending money to save money never went down well with the American consumer. This explained why diesel cars were popular in North America only when gas prices were sky high. It was the same story with non Japanese econoboxes after 1974.

Basically, something the American buyer would only undertake upon pain of death. Can you say Yugo? *Road & Track* described the situation in January 1977, when they lined up the Dasher hatchback against Japanese liftbacks the Toyota Celica and the Plymouth Arrow captive import.

Similarly equipped, and with a much smaller engine than the Celica and Arrow, the Dasher was up to a grand pricier, and *R&T* had this to say, "We thought it would make an interesting comparison to the two Japanese cars, but in reality it isn't. The Dasher is based on a different sort of philosophy than the other two and its basic problem is that few people in the US seem to feel the need to conserve fuel or natural resources." The journal also mentioned the steep Deutschmark was no friend to VW.

If only VW's new age cars were well built and reliable. It was a touchstone quality mentioned by Bud Lindemann, concerning a reason to buy the VW 412. However, it seemed this traditional mainstay had deserted Wolfsburg by the mid '70s. As VW scrambled to overcome red ink, introduce a raft of new models and replace the Beetle, it threw the baby out with the bath water, as the saying goes. Even auto historian Graham Robson, while acknowledging the Passat's virtues, noted it was no Beetle when it came to durability and quality.[11] However, maybe this didn't matter anymore?

It seemed the new generation of VWs were being bought by a different demographic compared to traditional VW buyers. The nature of the change was indicated by *Road & Track*'s February 1976 VW Dasher & Audi Fox Owner Survey. The journal prefaced its findings by stating the two cars

Volkswagen has never been in better shape.

The new VW412. For 1973.

A sleek new shape to take you into 1973. Now the big Volkswagen has good looks to go with all the other good features that made it such a popular range.

Sculptured profile. The new VW 412 (Four-one-two) bonnet curves smoothly and rakishly down at the front.

The Head-light surrounds. Designed to blend in with the new, aggressively styled nose.

The bonnet lines, headlight area and nose, plus a flaring over the wheel arches, all combine to give the VW 412 its attractive shape.

Interior restyling too. An elegant new wood-grain dashboard faces you. Another luxury touch for the big 412.

Fuel injection throughout the range. The new VW 412, Sedan and Variant, has the most advanced fuel system in the world. Electronic Fuel Injection. Split second metering in all driving conditions. To give more horsepower, snappier acceleration, lower maintenance costs and better fuel consumption.

Automatic power. Link Volkswagen's Automatic transmission with the fuel injection system and lively performance is the result. A sit back and relax automatic to smooth out city traffic.

A boot under the bonnet. Underneath our stylish bonnet you'll find a cavernous 400 dm³ (14 cu ft)

of boot space. With room for five average sized suitcases.

Even more storage space. The new VW 412 Variant has all the station wagon space you need — and more if

the back seat is folded down. The carpeted loading area also doubles as a romping room for kids.

Roominess is only half the story. Not only is the new VW 412 a big car, it's also a Volkswagen. Which means you get Volkswagen engineering and reliability with the best in saloon car luxury, and finish.

Service by Computer. This socket is built into every new VW 412, ready for when VW's Diagnostic Maintenance and Service System becomes computerised. Your car will be plugged into a computer which will print out a report on the health of the car. With the computer, Diagnosis time will be cut by a third.

Rely on Volkswagen to keep the new shape VW 412 in good shape

VW 412

WITH ELECTRONIC FUEL INJECTION

Volkswagens are made for keeps.

were dual purpose sports/economy sedans. Indeed, there seemed to be an element of this in Europe too, where the subsequent Golf GTi and its hot hatch ilk sounded the death knell for the traditional British sports car.

In Europe the family man desired the sporty two-seaters of his youth with the practicality of a hatch. Replace the MGB and VW 412, with a GTi? It seemed so for many families. This drive towards sports and utility kind of explained why the VW Scirocco was always overshadowed by the Golf. The story was similar in America. *R&T*'s survey put reasons for purchase as follows: economy 74%, handling 41%, performance 32%, front-drive 27%, styling 25% and interior space 20%. Economy was no surprise when it came to VW, but the reasons were slightly different. In the wake of the fuel crisis, fuel-efficient cars were much in demand.

Back in the Beetle days, great VW gas mileage was part of low cost economy car ownership. The big picture included low vehicle price and insurance premiums. By the mid '70s economy cars were bought mainly because they saved big time on newly expensive OPEC oil derived diesel and gasoline. VW Group's new water-cooled front-drivers weren't cheap to buy, but did save on newly pricey gasoline and diesel. The handling bug was also biting for all size and price classes in America. As horsepower went south with smog controls, the average buyer became increasingly preoccupied with slalom course speeds and lateral g-force skid pad readings. They were the new bragging rights ¼ mile times.

Just having front-wheel drive was a sales asset in its own right, even more so in America than Europe. In America it was a sign of modernity, in Europe it

was more desired for practical aspects like weight saving, winter traction and space utilization, if combined with a transverse engine. Concerning space utilization, the presence of a hatchback was probably just as key in buyers' minds, as a transverse, front-drive layout. Cars like the Mazda GLC/323 and Ford/Mercury Capri II were rear-drive, live-axled machines with luggage hatches. They were popular on both sides of the Atlantic. During the customer clinic phase, American Motors asked potential buyers if they would pay a premium for a front-drive version of its upcoming Pacer hatchback. The interest was limited. It seemed rear-drive or no, the key thing was that hatchback format. An ominous sign for future SUV popularity.

Here, South African assembled 412s come off the Uitenhage line in 1974. The factory would soon go water-cooled, and make the Mk1 Golf for years after production ended in Europe. (Courtesy Volkswagen South Africa)

A top of the line UK spec 1974 412LS Variant, with hi po AN dual carb 1800, is shown. (Courtesy David Botterill)

A crucial point of survey divergence with past air-cooled VWs was quality and reliability. Very few VW Dasher buyers mentioned VW quality, reliability or the extensive North American VW service network as reasons for buying their car. They were the reasons people bought Beetles in the past, and Datsuns and Toyotas in the present mid '70s. These new VW owners were younger, more willing to overlook the water-cooled car's reliability problems, and were quite taken by the VW front-driver's efficient manner.

Audi Fox owners were somewhat more miffed by the absence of quality and reliability they had expected from a prestige marque. However, VW buyers of the badge-engineered Dasher were more willing to roll with the recalls. In the words of a 25-year-old student, "It is the best combination of space, performance, economy and price available today. Love the car!" Out of the mouths of babes indeed. There had been a fundamental change in the VW buyer profile. After the Second World War, the average car buyer in Europe and the economy car buyer in America set great store by dependability, durability and general no nonsense, practical car ownership. This was certainly represented by the Beetle, and the motoring values possessed by the 411 and 412.

Thirty years after WWII, Europe was largely rebuilt. The Continent's average car buyer was now more affluent, compared to previous

The 120mph speedo was a bit overkill, but the 412 was a genuine 100mph car. The wood inlay dash reflected the class luxury found in a Ford Cortina Ghia. However, the VW 412 was much better made. (Courtesy David Botterill)

generations. They had no need, nor desire, to keep a car for ten years or, God forbid, said the car company … even longer! VW, Fiat, Renault and GM and Ford's European offshoots were all in the full grip of consumer fever by the '70s.

In America, too, it seemed consumerism had finally caught up with VW. Their old 'thrifty is nifty' style ads, and even Volvo's 'The eleven year car,' weren't resonating with the prototype yuppie 'Now Generation.' All this probably explained the VW 412's lukewarm reception at a time when the flashy VW Sports Bug was flying out of showrooms.

Pizzazz wasn't in Heinz Nordhoff's vocabulary, nor that of the traditional VW fancier. VW buyers used to be like Volvo Amazon and 140 buyers, except with a smaller car, at a lower price point. That traditional VW devotee was found by *VW Motoring*'s Aongus MacCana at the Beetle's Reunion air-cooled VW meet, held in Limerick Ireland in June 1992. One proud owner of a 175,000 mile 1969 Beetle 1200 was lady farmer Mary Lonergan. The Beetle had been owned by Lonergan since new, and was now a

solid condition 23-year-old Bug.

Then there was a 1973 Beetle 1303S, that is a Super Beetle 1600 with curved windshield and safety dashboard. This sedan was purchased by policeman John O'Riordan as a used car in 1981 with 70,000 miles on the odometer. Ten years later the Super Beetle was on 220,000 miles, and hadn't needed a major overhaul. So, VW owners were value conscious people that held on to their cars for a number of years.[12]

By the mid-70s it seemed the modern buyer was willing to pay a premium for efficiency, during a shorter duration of car ownership. However, the value for money question was hard to overlook. The qualities of subcompact size and thrift could be bought for $1000 less than a Dasher, with a Japanese import. For a grand more, a luxury domestic intermediate V8 personal car. In the same year that *Car and Track* got 33mpg out of its Dasher, it got 12mpg from a Mercury Cougar XR7 460 V8, and Olds Cutlass Salon 350 V8. The latter had a factory handling kit that made cornering reasonably controlled, if not in the virtual sports car class of the Dasher. A 10mpg V8 personal car,

A Blaupunkt Frankfurt stereo radio and VDO gauges. All from the days when German cars used German brand equipment, made in West Germany. (Courtesy David Botterill)

20mpg VW 412, or 30mpg Dasher … the choice was yours.

Unlike the Dasher, both V8 chariots avoided a buckboard ride, and were great highway cruisers. Being larger than the Dasher, VW's 412 had arrived with four-door convenience in 1973 at $3300. Unlike Dasher, the 412 had standard fuel-injection. This eradicated the drivability problems of early carb fed, Audi-engined Dashers and Rabbits. Even in 1974 the compact-sized, more family-orientated 412, could be purchased cheaper at a dealer than the Dasher.

The trouble was the car-buying public had always been demographically compartmentalized. The result was that the 412's overall abilities were overlooked. Domestic buyers stayed with home grown, and Japanese import prospects were loyal to their Datsuns and Toyotas. It was unlikely one of the young buyers in America that typically went with a Dasher would have considered the very able and well made VW 412.

Following VW tradition, the Type 4 continued its evolutionary path. The new 1973 412 had wiper arms in black, not silver. It was the kind of VW revision that would have occupied several column inches in *Der Spiegel* at one time! 1973 was the last year that the Type 4's parking light indicator lived within the speedometer. It also marked the end of having two separate turn signal left and right warning lights. 1974 saw a single turn signal indicator, within the clock face. 1974 North American 412s also saw less welcome VW additions.

VW 412 1974 AD
'Interlock' was a federally mandated logic sequence computer, fitted to all North American sold cars in 1974. It made front seat occupants buckle

up before the car could be started. Unfortunately, it wasn't always reliable, or precise. So the engine wouldn't start sometimes, even if seatbelts were used. A light bag of groceries placed on the passenger seat was enough to stop the engine starting. Under pressure from automakers and the public, Interlock only lasted six months. However, the mandatory 5mph front and rear impact bumpers were here to stay.

It's a shame the Type 4's final year saw Interlock and the big impact bumpers. The equivalent bumpers on the Dasher, Scirocco and Golf were much neater, due to their upright grilles. The 412's front fascia leant forward, so the bumper had to protrude further. Plus, with only one year left in the model cycle, a major impact bumper redesign wasn't forthcoming. Fortunately, Interlock and impact bumpers didn't apply in Europe. Indeed, European spec 412s also benefited from that continent's freer pollution laws.

In a universal move for all markets, the 412 went to an 1800 Type 4 flat-four for '74 MY. The 1.8-liter motor represented a 93mm bore out, of the preceding 1700. This 1795cc (93 x 66mm) 412 motor was also shared with the VW-Porsche 914 and Type 2 Bus in 1974 and 1975. However, there were detailed specification differences. The lo po Bus application was even more directed towards torque. The Bus cylinder heads had 39mm intake valves and 33mm exhaust valves. There was better breathing on the 914 and 412, with respective valve sizes of 41mm and 34mm.

The VW-Porsche and 412 had their case stamped engine numbers in different locations. There was also a lower oil dipstick tube mounting for Variants, compared to the 914.

Concerning 412LS nomenclature, 'L' stood for Deluxe, and the 'S' for the most powerful motor in the range. By late 1974 a Volvo 145DL was £2123. As a medium-sized European wagon, this VW 412LS could have been yours for just £1658 … and it was faster than previous models! (Courtesy David Botterill)

One of only ten remaining 1974 VW 412LS Variants in Germany. (Courtesy Hilmar Walde)

Of greater note were differences in compression ratio and carburetion, between North America and ROW markets. North America stayed with fuel-injection for 1974, due to tightening pollution laws. Indeed, the North American Bug would adopt fuel-injection for 1975. However, with less draconian laws, European 1974 412s were all on carbs, with two states of tune.

For Europe the base 1800 had a 7.8:1 CR and made 75bhp at five grand, and 95lb/ft at 3400rpm. Four-speed stick 412s could now hurl to 93mph, with 0-100km/h in 16.5 seconds. Equivalent factory figures for the automatic 412 were 91mph and 20 seconds. Such 412s were denoted 412, or 412L for the Deluxe edition.

The hi po 1800's dual Solex 40 PDSTT carbs worked with an 8.6:1 CR for 85bhp at 5000rpm and a useful 100lb/ft at 3400rpm. Manual 412s were good for 98mph and 0-100km/h in 14.5 seconds, with the automatic version capable of 96mph and 17.5 seconds for 0-100km/h.

Those still in the market for a Type 4 would have noticed it was becoming an even livelier sedan. It was faster now, with carbs, than the previous injection model. This, combined with all the other evolutionary 411/412 refinements over the years, had produced a fine family car. To borrow a line from American Motors, it wasn't getting older, it was getting better! Indeed, almost as fleet of foot as a BMW. To fight the fuel crisis and hard economic times that followed, the Bavarians introduced their 1.8-liter, 90 horse 518 four-speed.

The BMW's 99mph top speed and 0-100km/h time of 13.9 seconds was virtually the same as the hi po 'S' suffixed 412 cars. Sizewise they were also in the same ballpark. The VW 412 was 180.4in long and 64.4in wide, with BMW's 518 on a respective 181.9in and 66.5in. However, in reality, the VW's interior was roomier, with the rear-engined nature a boon for true three-seater, rear bench accommodation. Then too, the 412S's 98mph top speed was also its cruising speed, in Wolfsburg's fine tradition. Pricing saw the VW and BMW poles apart, in spite of comparable quality.

By the close of production the UK spec 412LS four-door was £1605, and by the time the BMW 518 reached Britain in 1975 it was £3459, and the 412 was gone, although during 1974 there was a time window when both cars were available in Continental Europe. In February 1974 the West German market VW 412L four-door was DM 10,995, with the 412LS on DM 11,145. Even though the 412's specification and abilities were comparable to luxury rivals, it was unlikely model comparisons would have been entertained outside the opining of car magazines.

The car market in Europe was as demographically divided as America, then and now. In late '70s Germany a company representative would get a contract if he turned up in a Mercedes or BMW, but never an Opel Senator. So it would seem not even the VW-Porsche 914's usage of the high output 85bhp 1800 would have helped the VW 412. As ever, a VW was a VW. In North America, 1974 412s were running with a single 50 state, emissions okay 1800 Type 4 powerplant. In 1973 California, the Golden State, had the 'smogged-down' 72bhp 1700, with the 49 state edition on 80 horse. VW split the difference for 1974, with a Bosch L-jetronic fuel-injected 76bhp (SAE net) 1800 motor.

In 1974 it was back to carbs in Europe, and the 'S' in 412LS indicated the hi po 85bhp 1800. (Courtesy Hilmar Walde)

This 1974 VW 412LS Variant's color is the factory original L20A Marino Yellow. (Courtesy Hilmar Walde)

The luxurious interior of the 412LS Variant. The only VW more expensive was the NSU-designed VW K70. (Courtesy Hilmar Walde)

Emissions control favored a switch from Bosch D-jetronic to the second generation L-jet system, with the latter working on airflow (the German word for air started with 'L' – Luft). An airflow meter with a moveable door admitted intake air. The door's position would be relayed via a potentiometer to the injection system's ECU, as an electronic signal. The computer then worked out the optimal duration for the injector solenoids to stay open.

The Bosch L-jet system was a little less problematic than D-jet. By operating on airflow it was less sensitive to engine wear issues, but could still be tripped up by vacuum leaks. So, incorrectly sealed intake and exhaust manifold gaskets, or even an improperly seated oil dipstick, could introduce vacuum leaks that invited rough running and hard starting, through too lean a mixture.

Indeed, the whole lean tuning business, to clean up emissions and please the EPA, wasn't cool for air-cooled Volkswagens. In the absence of a radiator the air-cooled motor relied greatly on engine oil for heat transference. Along similar lines a relatively rich fuel mixture also overcame the lack of a radiator. Those cooling fins couldn't do it alone! So VW's air-cooled flat fours didn't much care for lean tuning.

With Bosch electronic fuel-injected cars of this era, cold starts were aided by an extra injector. The cold start injector acted like an automatic choke. Although Bosch L-jet was fitted to many different cars all over the globe, including the 1975-77 North American Beetle, the 412 had a unique airflow meter, that has introduced an unobtainium issue in recent times.

It should be noted that for the first couple of months of the 1974 North American model year, delivered 412s still sported Bosch D-jetronic. In addition, even when L-jet made its debut, 412s and 914s still retained their 1700 era D-jet camshaft profiles. This old cam wasn't suited in terms of correct fuel mixture. It all brought complaints of mediocre performance and hot running. 1974 North American

412s adopted the lower 7.8:1 CR, seen on European base engined 1974 412s. This was a come down from the 8.2:1 CR seen on previous North American Type 4s, and was also a factor in poor engine response.

There are some inconsistencies between parts book theory and reality, concerning Type 4 motors. For connecting rod numbers a 021 prefix was thought to concern carburettor engines. However, such prefixed parts have been seen in America, on the injected 411 and Type 2 Bus. In addition, the 022 prefix for injection engines has been considered to be the correct prefix for 1800 Type 4 connecting rods, as seen on 1974-75 412/Bus models. In practice such 022 prefix connecting rods, with 24mm pins, have also been noticed on earlier 1700s.

The engine number Z prefix concerns early 411s, and wasn't witnessed on North American Type 4 cases. From observations in the field, the start of T4 availability in North America saw parts sharing with the T2 Bus. VW could have done a better fuel system, engine tuning job on '74 412s for North America. However, figuring the 412 and Porsche 914 were coming to a close, they probably didn't think it was worth it. It all seems to make the pre-impact bumper, 80bhp, 49-state 412s of 1973, the more desirable of stock condition collectibles.

For 1975 the Type 4 1800 motor lived on in the 914 and T2 Bus. Sadly, apocalyptic federal law saw pesky smog controls make their presence felt, as the Muskie Smog Bill became reality. This implied standard air injection (smog pump), and selective use of EGR (exhaust gas recirculation) on 49-state 914s and T2s. Golden State 914s also added insult to injury with a catalytic converter, so no lead from now on.

The engine the VW 412 should have had in North America was the 2-liter edition of the Type 4 motor. This unit was a Porsche exclusive during 1973-75. Given CAFE hadn't arrived yet, and VW had the Bug for fuel misers, there wasn't a reason why the American 412 couldn't have this smog legal, 100bhp (net), fuel-injected powerplant. Returning to the precedent of late 1940s history, Porsche had taken a VW motor, the Type 4 1700, and developed a high-performance version. Zuffenhausen did this, because it required a replacement engine for the 2-liter Porsche 911 mill, used in the expensive and slow selling Porsche 914/6.

Porsche took that 411 1700, and added a 71mm stroker crank, new connecting rod bearings and bigger 94mm pistons. Porsche's Type 4 2-liter casing was stronger, and better finished. The motor's crankshaft had wider spaced journals, and was treated to make it harder. Both qualities strengthened the bottom end, making it suitable for turbocharging. Sadly, VW and Porsche never tried a turbo on the Type 4 flat-four, at the factory level. Also handy for turbocharging was the 2-liter unit's sodium filled valves. This flat-four also sported better flowing heads and higher quality pistons, compared to VW 411s and VW-Porsche 914 1.7/1.8-liter motors.

Porsche's 2-liter Type 4 motor kept the 1700's Bosch D-jet fuel-injection, but the injectors had larger capacity than the units in 411/412s and 914 1.7Ls. The Porsche 914 2.0 held on to its 100bhp (net) power rating in 1974. However, due to tighter smog laws in 1975, the motor dropped five horses. By 1976 the 2-liter was down to 86bhp net, and was shared by the 914 2.0 and entry level 911, called 912E. The latter had Bosch L-jet fuel-injection. By

This 1974 Swedish spec 412 automatic with power brakes was originally a police car from the town of Pitea. (Courtesy Kharon8)

1976 the 914 1.8L was history, and the 914 was only sold in North America. The Porsche 912E was for America only, also.

By 1976 the Porsche 914 2.0, 912E and VW Type 2 Bus were the sole users of the Type 4 motor, all in 2-liter form. However, come 1977 and just the Type 2 was using this flat-four. At the same hour, the final model year 1977 Beetle sedan Stateside utilized a 48bhp Bosch L-jet version of the Type 1 motor, in 1600 form. The Type 2 Bus kept on using the VW 411/412's Type 4 motor, in 2-liter form, through 1979. The next generation Vanagon then adopted said Type 4 2-liter mill through mid-1983. At this point the Vanagon switched to the Wasserboxer flat-four. This unit was a modified Type 1 motor, which utilized water cooling and a conventional radiator system. Some final refinements for the Type 4 motor were hydraulic lifters in 1978, and electronic ignition for 1979. So, the Type 4 allowed the final T2 VW Buses to enjoy reduced maintenance.

The Type 4's hardware also made it to the racing world, both on- and off-road. Formula Vee, with its Type 1-powered single-seater open wheelers, was a similar entry level avenue to motor racing, like Formula Ford. A step up from this was Formula Super Vee, 1970s open wheeler racing that permitted the more powerful Type 4 motor, with its greater durability and build up potential. Formula Super Vee also permitted the 411's rear semi-trailing arm, independent suspension to become part of the single seater chassis.[13]

In off-road racing, the suitcase Type 4 motor, where the cooling fan mounts to the crankshaft, found great usage in terms of the Porsche 912E unit. This 2-liter Type 4 flat-four had freer flowing heads, and with larger barrels could go to 2.6 liters! Indeed, by the early 1980s the Type 4 had taken over from the T1 2180cc unit, as the racer's off-road VW motor of choice. While the Type 1 motor had been a more accessible, cheaper route for off-road racing, the specialized, high-end area of the sport made use of the Type 4 engine's superior durability.[14]

With enough folding stuff, the T4

As with all Swedish spec Type 4s, this 412 came with power brakes. However, it was also delivered with the optional 85bhp 1800 dual carb AN motor. (Courtesy Kharon8)

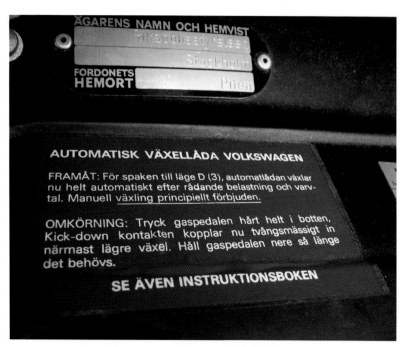

Swedish proof of this 412 four-door sedan's police force past. Instructions also explain safe usage of the automatic gearbox; a rare option in 1974 Europe. (Courtesy Kharon8)

motor can produce higher outputs more reliably than its T1 counterpart. It all depends on the extent a racer is prepared to go. To reduce the weight of the T4 motor, in relation to the T1 powerplant, aftermarket fiberglass pieces can be used to replace the T4's stock cooling tinwork. This can reduce the weight disadvantage between the 411 and Beetle engines to just 40lb. So the power build up potential can be enjoyed without the weight penalty. Indeed, in the world of racing and cars in general, success is all about recognizing potential and using it.

The Type 4 411/412's story seems to have been of a worthy car, overlooked by the public. A public for which conventional styling and convenience items, have always been an easier sell. The Beetle bucked this trend by going full scale puritan, and profited for 25 years by doing so. However, in higher market segments the 24/7 reliability story didn't play so well. Prestige and perception don't work well with logic. Towards the

end in 1974, the 412LS Variant was £1658, and a Volvo 145DL was £2123. As a sedan the Volvo 144DL was good for 90mph, 0-60mph in 13.9 seconds and 23.5mpg, according to *Autocar*. The VW 412LS was a similar size, quicker and slightly more economical. It seemed like a bargain, if a buyer was looking for a bargain. However, somehow the Type 4 got lost in the European middle sector crowd.

Coming into 1974, VW was trying to stay on the straight and narrow, in more ways than one. VW Group was going for self-centering steering, or negative kingpin offset, to be precise. With a negative steering offset, the center of the tire to road footprint was now inside the steering pivot axis. *Car and Track* gave a TV demonstration using a '74 Super Beetle, where the car tracked straight when braking on two different surfaces. If a tire blew out, the steering geometry would steer the car in the opposite direction to the skid, keeping the vehicle on a safe path. VW Dasher ads saw the system denoted as the 'Skidbreaker.'

On the subject of safety, VWoA was having some difficulties with the NHTSA and 'Nader's Raiders,' or The Center For Auto Safety, concerning the Type 181. The Type 181 (or Thing), had been getting around the usual passenger car safety requirements, by being classified as a 'multipurpose passenger vehicle.' The main bones of contention were the close proximity of the windshield to the front occupants, and the lack of a rollover structure. Concerning the latter, the fold down windshield offered zero protection.

The government and safety lobby challenged the contention that The Thing was even a multipurpose vehicle, under current legislation. More than this, there was a proposal

to amend the exemption, so that multipurpose vehicles were only truck-based. As things transpired The Thing continued on sale into 1975. According to some publications it garnered the same Bosch L-jet injected 1600 as Beetle. It seems more likely they were left over carb fed '74s. Common sense would have dictated fitting the dealer option rollbar structure to The Thing, regardless of government regs – *Pickup Van & 4 Wheel Drive* magazine said as much in January 1975. By being in possession of electronic fuel-injection, self-centering steering, and a roof, the VW 412 seemed a complete package. However, the winds of change were blowing against air-cooled VWs.

TYPE 4 – LAST OF THE AIR-COOLED VWS, FIRST OF A NEW WAVE ...

When the VW 411 was on the drawing board, and on release, Volkswagen AG was the third biggest automaker in the world. It was famous for being a purveyor of rear-engined air-cooled vehicles. At that point in time, with VW reaching a sales zenith in North America, there seemed no reason why this would change anytime soon. VW were diversifying into other brands and formats, but the old air-cooled, rearward ways still seemed commercially sound. However, six years hence, as the VW 412 was winding down, Volkswagen was well on the way to a new front-drive future. The Beetle was about to start a four year

A roof antenna and re-upholstered seats were police force changes. This VW 412 moved to Finland in the late '80s, when the town of Pitea sold it as a retired cop car. (Courtesy Kharon8)

You can still get there in luxury.

Despair not.
Though the road to Granny's grows longer as the gasoline supply grows shorter, you can still make it. And elegantly, at that.
In a luxury Volkswagen.
The VW 412. Which needs less gas to go more miles. (What else?) Granny will surely commend you

for your good sense.
And your good taste.
For a luxury 412 comes replete with the expected amenities.
Room. Plush seats. Thick carpets. Big windows. Flo-thru ventilation. And some unexpected amenities. Steel-belted radials. Electronic fuel injection. A timed preheater.

Front disc brakes. Metallic paint. All standard.
Plus our unique Owner's Security Blanket with Computer Analysis.
So, with a luxury four-door Volkswagen, you can still get all the nice things you're used to.
Including Granny's apple pie.

Volkswagen's luxury 412

This 1974 ad shows the new federally mandated impact bumpers, and mentions the recent fuel crisis. Luxurious economy cars were quickly finding favor. (Courtesy Volkswagen AG)

phase out move, as far as European production was concerned.

As much as the Type 4 seems representative of VW's 1938-1973 era, it was in reality a transitionmobile to Wolfsburg's new future. Under that Big Bug Body were engineering clues that didn't require Hercule Poirot to follow. Unitary construction, electronic fuel-injection, MacPherson strut front, semi-trailing arm rear suspension and fully automatic transmission would eventually all be found on a VW Rabbit or Golf near you soon.

Given all the above originated on the rear-engined, air-cooled Type

3 and 4, it is hard to understand *Road & Track*'s February 1975 contention that VW was a behind-the-times contender in pre Passat days, "… and has progressed from a technologically backward company to a highly competent one in less than a decade." It is strange that this accusation was never leveled at Porsche, quite the contrary. When it came to Zuffenhausen, Porsche were chastised for making anything but the 911, and was repeatedly told by anyone drawing breath to keep making those rear-engined, air-cooled, anti-styling two-door cars, that some said looked an awful lot like a Beetle! More than that, Porsche was looked upon, as representing the height of West German technological modernity for doing so.

In 1975 much of Detroit was still wedded to cast iron, the separate chassis, live axle and carburettor. VW had been doing light alloy and independent suspension since the 1930s. In 1975, the Beetle and Thing, according to *Road & Track*, rear-engined and air-cooled as they were, were the only VWs sold in North America with electronic fuel-injection. [15] The modern Dasher, Rabbit and Scirocco all used one two-barrel Zenith carb to feed their drivability-challenged Audi four bangers. The VW 411/412 had new things to offer, if one was prepared to look. The Type 4 also had some old things from VW's past that were also desirable.

A high quality, well constructed car of compact size, with good snowbelt winter traction, and no boil over radiator, still made sense in 1975. Indeed, although the Type 4 was officially at an end by the close of '74 MY, 51 additional 412 Variants were made through March 1975. However, in the normal course of VW business, it had long been decided for the 412 to move over at Wolfsburg for the new Golf.

Many at the time were looking forward to this new start at VW. From motoring journalists, to Wolfsburg assembly line workers and VW dealers. However, the VW air-cooled, rear-engined legacy has remained strong ever since. It even stayed in production in South America into the 21st Century. Indeed, the current wasser boxer 911 at Porsche in Zuffenhausen maintains the design legacy of Dr Porsche's Beetle. For those not wishing to worry about torque vectoring front differentials, or cooling system leaks, the VW 411/412, along with their air-cooled brethren, provide an oasis of relief. They hailed from those pre recall ridden times, when the snowplow operator got to work thanks to VW.

1. Mag-type Wheel Covers.
The racy look of mag wheels, at a fraction of their cost. Five wide spokes, simulated wheel lugs and raised hub make these covers look like the real thing. Aluminum finish is resistant to rust and corrosion.

2. Side Slat Grille.
This anodized aluminum grille dresses up the side vents of your 4-Door. Snaps on quickly, easily, securely.

Volkswagen's Sublime-to-the-Ridiculous Sale

The Sublime VW 412
Our luxury 412 comes equipped with fuel injection, 4-wheel independent suspension, automatic transmission, steel-belted radials, plush seats and thick carpeting—all at no extra cost. On top of all this, your VW dealer is prepared to offer you substantial savings on his remaining '74 models.

The Ridiculous VW Thing
We've just reduced the price of the Volkswagen Thing from $3150 to $2775.* What's a Thing? The car that can be anything. The doors come off, the top goes up or down (the windshield, too), and it has an air-cooled rear engine that gives you the traction you need to go just about anywhere.

(Participating dealers only.)

*Thing (181) East Coast P.O.E., suggested retail price. (West Coast slightly higher.) Local taxes and other dealer delivery charges additional. ©Volkswagen of America, Inc.

Top right: The Type 4 could be personalized with factory mag covers and chrome vents. The rear 5mph impact bumper shows this is a 1974 US spec 412 sedan. (Courtesy Volkswagen AG)

Right: VW called the 412 sublime and the Type 181 ridiculous. It was technically the final year for both in North America, and VW dealers were offering big discounts on remaining '74 MY stock. The Rabbit was coming. (Courtesy Volkswagen AG)

VW – A COMPANY
IN TRANSITION

HERBIE RIDES AGAIN

In 1974 *Car and Track* took another look at the inimitable VW Beetle. This time it was in the form of a yellow Super Beetle (1303S) for the American market. Bud Lindemann noted that it was the best Beetle yet, in terms of being tougher and plusher. However, Lindemann and others felt even the Super Beetle might not be enough to turn around Wolfsburg's fortunes, saying, "However, not the panacea VW needs to hi po their sales charts." The fact was stated that VW's American sales had fallen from 569,000 in 1970 to 253,000 in 1973.

The *Car and Track* evaluation saw 0-60mph in 18.5 seconds, and 70mph to zero in 166 neat feet. The former was around 2.5 seconds off the pace of the Beetle's contemporary Japanese econobox rivals. That said, the braking result was exceptional for the era. Straightline stops in a short distance, with minimal brake fade or nose dive was hard to comprehend, given the North American Bug's retention of its familiar four-wheel

drums! The rest of the test seemed a foregone conclusion.

The Super Beetle snaked through slalom cones like a sports car compared to domestic barges, but was noisy and cramped. It also didn't exactly ride like the proverbial cloud. In a mix of all kinds of driving, the Super Beetle got a flat 27mpg. This included flat out running on Grattan Raceway, by a pro racing driver. In the end even this new and improved Bug, with Nader-placating curved windshield, safety dashboard and flow-through ventilation, seemed an underpowered and uncomfortable car. Indeed, Lindemann offered this conclusion, "The little ugly bug has had its day in the American sun. Now enter the Squareback, 412 and the Dasher to keep Volkswagen's hopes alive."

In truth, much the same had been said about VWs since the early 1940s. British automaker Humber also felt the VW was underpowered and unexceptional, when assessing a captured Kübelwagen during World War II; its assessment didn't alter when

The mid-engined EA266 Beetle successor was designed by Ferdinand Piëch. It was spotted in Lapland, escorted by two Super Bug bodyguards! (Courtesy CAR & Syme Magazines)

observing a Beetle after it. Nothing to see here, they told the British government, concerning a ground-breaking design for the British auto industry to study. Thirty years later, it seemed commentators in Britain and Europe echoed Bud Lindemann's Bug glumness. For UK TV's *Drive In* car show, Richard Hudson Evans introduced the new VW Golf to the British public, and made mention of VW's long serving Beetle.

Hudson Evans noted that even with 18 million Beetles produced by late 1974, and the Golf's arrival, VW had stated that the Bug would live on for some time yet. He also said that Wolfsburg, once the main domicile of the beloved Beetle, was now the province of the new Golf. Mention was made of the Golf's four introductory versions, the 1100 standard and deluxe (L) and the equivalent Audi-engined 1500 editions. Meanwhile, the Beetle was "… now banished to a north seaside satellite plant instead."

The satellite plant referred to Emden, the long standing Beetle supply factory

for America. Rabbits would also be made there as the Beetle ran down in terms of European production. All of this was prior to the establishment of VW's Westmoreland facility in 1978. Belgian journalist and racer Paul Frère also discussed the Beetle when introducing the Golf to *Road & Track* readers in its August 1974 issue. Frère said caution should be exercised in speaking of a Beetle successor – many false dawns had come in earlier times. That said, concerning the Golf/Rabbit, he noted it was "… probably the one to take over the Beetle's role."

Restating VW's current late 1974 position, Paul Frère said Wolfsburg management was adamant that Golf production wouldn't interfere with the Bug's program. Much was said of VW's fall from grace in 1974, whereupon the company posted its first ever loss. The figure was DM 807,000,000 in the red. Beetle production in West Germany had sunk to 451,800 in the wake of the first fuel crisis and ensuing global recession. The previous year had seen the widest Beetle range ever, with the

The Type 3 ended in 1973, making way for the VW Passat. Likewise, the 412 was through at the end of '74 MY, giving the Golf Wolfsburg space. However, the Beetle soldiered on at Emden into 1978. (Courtesy Mot)

1303's arrival. 1973 model year also witnessed the final times for the Type 3, and the start of production of the new VW 412.

In spite of all the above, VW's scheme to go Passat, Scirocco, Golf and Polo was well advanced. The VW Golf was shown to the West German press in May 1974. The final Wolfsburg-made Beetle alighted in July 1974. VW planned Golf production at 3000 units per day, for the fall of 1974. That was the same production rate as the Beetle in its spring/summer times at Wolfsburg that same year. The Beetle was a convenient scapegoat for VW's problems, but the Lil' Bug was still selling strongly globally. From 1965 through 1973, except for 1967, worldwide Beetle production exceeded one million units per annum.

Even in recessionary 1974, Beetle production still reached 791,053 units. Paul Frère said 1974 production still saw the Beetle at 5000 units per day globally. He also said that the Beetle, due to its big sales volume, was still the only car that VW made a profit on. This was something even the new popular Passat couldn't claim. People were buying fewer Beetles and other air-cooled VWs in 1974. However, in the aftermath of the fuel crisis, the world was buying less of everything. Even BMW was in the red during the second half of the financial year.

Even though Bug model versions were pruned, as the water-cooled iterations arrived, 1975 Britain was limited to the non Super Beetle 1200/1600 and ragtop, the sales were still amassing. Famously in February 1972, and much to Henry's chagrin, the Beetle reached 15,007,034 total sales. It was enough to knock off ye olde Model T as the all time sales champ. Ford found another million Model Ts, but at Emden in October 1974 the 18 millionth Beetle rolled off the production line. After Wolfsburg stopped doing the Bug, European assembly of the evergreen small car continued at Emden, Hanover and Brussels in the 1974-78 era.

The 20 millionth Beetle was made on May 15 1981, as production in South America continued. Although scaled back, the Beetle stayed over 100,000 units per annum through 1984. It also got back to over 100,000 in 1994, reaching 115,656. Before that, the 21 millionth Beetle was made at the Mexican VW plant in Puebla on June 23 1992. For '93 MY, the Beetle's Type 1 motor was revised to accept an oil filter, fuel-injection (Electronic Digifant) and hydraulic lifters. All the features that were seen on the Type 4's flat-four, earlier on.

Brazilian Beetle production restarted in 1994 after going on hiatus in 1986. Indeed, in the mid-1990s there was discussion by VW management concerning bringing the Beetle back to Europe, as an official South American import, like in the 1979-85 era. Once again the Beetle would serve as an entry level VW, in European showrooms. A catalytic converter had been introduced on '91 MY Mexican Beetles, so emissions wouldn't be a problem in Europe. Crash safety was still the head-on 30mph barrier test, sans crash dummies, and only observing steering column intrusion.

The cost of developing a small car had been rising over the years, as European consumers desired more convenience gadgets. This was leaving room for a basic small car that buyers could afford as a new vehicle. In the end the plan didn't come to pass. The idea morphed into the late '90s arrival of the Golf-based New Beetle. The New Beetle was more of an upscale, niche boutique model. The coming of stricter European pollution and noise standards probably put an end to the

Type 1 Beetle's return as a mainstream European model. At the same time Porsche ended its original air-cooled 911, due to pending smog and drive-by noise laws also. However, all of the above didn't stop the original Bug living on in Puebla past the year 2000, with over 22 million units produced.

Some qualities connected with the Beetle's longevity were its solid, value for money dependability. Even in 1974, such features were apparent next to the new Passat. The Passat LS two-door 1500 cost £1417 and delivered 27.8mpg. The top trim Beetle 1303S with curved windshield, safety dash and 1600 motor was just £1005. Also tested by *Autocar* magazine, the 1303S consumed 27.4mpg overall; while the Passat could reach the high 90s in top speed, the Beetle could cruise at its low 80s top speed indefinitely. A 40% plus price increase was one heck of a surcharge for the Passat's extra space and turn of speed. The VW 411 and 412 were indeed an ultimate expression of the Beetle's traditional VW ideals. However, back in the late '60s, VW was truly at the proverbial crossroads.

A NEW BUSINESS PLAN
In 1969 Dr Kurt Lotz was looking for more profit, Volkswagen shareholders expected it. Dr Lotz found it, partly by making Ferry Porsche pay the full economic price on 914 bodies. Not the 'gentleman's agreement' price agreed between Ferry and Heinz Nordhoff. Then there was the VW 411, Lotz went ahead with the Type 4, rather than the smaller Type 5 311. The VW 411 was the largest and priciest Volkswagen so far. There would be good value-added potential here. The earnings of Volkswagen AG would also be bolstered if a Beetle replacement could be found.

In searching for Herbie II, Dr Kurt Lotz embarked upon two avenues. The 1969 Turin Motor Show saw Lotz impressed with the work of Giorgetto Giugiaro. This led to the ItalDesign founder, being commissioned to do a VW concept car. Around the same time, Dr Lotz engaged the design services of Porsche. Zuffenhausen had come up with the first 'People's Car,' so why not the second? For a time this looked like being Project EA266. This was a rear-drive sedan, with mid-engine location. The transverse, water-cooled motor, would reside under the rear seat.

EA266 was the work of the great Ferdinand Piëch, who was still at Porsche. The prototype was spotted in Lapland, escorted by two VW Super Beetles. Indeed, the Super Beetle had also been launched on Dr Lotz's watch, and proved commercially successful. However, the VW K70 of 1970-75 was also in Dr Lotz's era, and this sedan didn't sell too well. It was decision time for VW. The K70's inability to set the European market on fire, fueled a reluctance on the part of Lotz and VW management to give up on rear-engined cars. Declining Beetle sales in North America, the Type 4's modest commercial achievements, and difficulties finding a Beetle replacement, all precipitated Dr Kurt

Sportscars and wagons were under siege from hatchbacks as the '70s wore on. (Author)

Lotz stepping down as VW CEO in October 1971.

Lotz's replacement was Rudolf Leiding. Leiding had joined VW just after the war, and was a rising star with successful leadership periods at VW do Brasil, and at Audi-NSU. It was Leiding that canned EA266. The mid-engined sedan would have just been too expensive to make. He also closed the door on rear-engined, air-cooled VWs. Observing the sales success of his 1972 Audi 80, he gave the go ahead for the VW clone known as Passat. This decision set VW on its front-drive, water-cooled path.

In July 1973, Karl Ludvigsen wrote a *Road & Track* article about the VW do Brasil sports car called SP-2. Ludvigsen asked VW do Brasil president Werner P Schmidt why VW wasn't making a jazzy little number like the SP-2 in Wolfsburg? Schmidt's response was, "I wish we had an answer that was as good as that question." Well, they did, but were unable to say it at the time. The coupe answer was Scirocco, one of the new wave VWs that would replace the Elvis jukebox era Karmann Ghia no less.

Of course VW's Ludwig Kraus was working on the new VW kit car system, of front-drive, water-cooled models. The reason he was doing so was because VW management, now led by Rudolf Leiding, felt the Beetle and its ilk were no longer viable in current financial or design terms. VWs had traditionally been low cost, high quality automobiles. However, quality costs money. A look at film footage of Beetles being made at Emden during 1975-77, showed that VW's traditional design had many parts and involved a labor intensive process. With the value of the Deutschmark climbing, and West German labor costs being much higher than was the case in Japan, the difficulty of profitably offering an inexpensive small family car, with a 24-month/24,000 mile warranty, became apparent. Something had to give.

EA266 was too pricey to make, and the early mid-'70s Golfs used cheap Eastern European steel. So did the Alfa Romeo Sud. As a result, not many of those early Golfs or Rabbits survive. Indeed, early Passats, Sciroccos, Golfs and Polos lacked the Beetle-like solidity that had made VW a byword for quality. As true as this was, the design of the new age VWs, and the magazine statistics they produced, were an easy sell to the European consumer. Buyers were looking for more space, more economy and performance from a small car in the wake of the fuel crisis. At a time when the average buyer was spending a large percentage of their disposable income to feed their daily driver, numbers mattered.

Those numbers were supplied by Rainer Guenzler's TV test for *Sportsspiegel* of a 1975 VW Scirocco TS. 'Der Autotest' showed Scirocco to be capable of 0-100km/h in 10.8 seconds and 9.7 liters per 100km. Such respective acceleration and economy figures were obtained with the 85bhp 1500 motor and four-speed. Equivalent figures for rivals the Ford Capri II 1600 and Opel Manta SR 1.6 were 13.6 seconds/12.5 liters per 100km and 13.8 seconds/12.2 liters per 100km. From these figures it became apparent why automakers on both sides of the Atlantic were going front-drive and transversely-engined for the eighties. Driveshafts added weight, and stole from interior packaging efficiency, even though Capri II was a liftback.

Paul Frère had introduced the Golf/Rabbit and the Karmann-built Scirocco to *Road & Track* readers.

By coincidence he had raced with Guenzler in the past. In the present, he too was talking up the efficiency benefits of reduced vehicle weight. Comparing European spec cars, a Golf 1500 was 250lb lighter than a Super Beetle 1600. The latter wasn't exactly a heavyweight at 1970lb! Frère remarked about getting nearly 100mph out of the Golf 1500 on VW's test track, and the importance of aerodynamics.

VW's latest proving grounds were completed in the early '70s, 15 miles north of Wolfsburg, on a 2620 acre site. Construction had started in 1967. It included a 12.5-mile high speed oval, the track that Frère tried the Golf on. Next to this track, was the largest wind tunnel in Europe, also completed around this time. Aerodynamics and weight saving would prove crucial in a post fuel crisis environment. UK *Drive In* TV presenter Richard Hudson Evans said that advanced, innovative engineering, like the canned mid-engined EA266, was likely to become less common in such times. There would be a drive to the conventional car, as per the VW Golf that *Drive In* was evaluating.

Indeed, a front-drive, transversely-engined car was nothing new. Austin and Fiat had earlier examples. The 1971 Fiat 127 even sported a hatchback. So, it seemed less likely that ground-breaking designs, such as the VW Beetle, Citroën DS or NSU Ro80, would arrive in the future. Corporate survival dictated honing fuel and space efficiency, with conventional cars. However, there seemed a price tag for the efficiency gains through such small, lightweight hatchbacks. Paul Frère said the 30mph frontal type approval crash test was easily passed by the new Golf. That said, this test wasn't particularly strict.

The subcompact Golf showed a

Under Dr Kurt Lotz, it was thought that front drive, water-cooled Audis and rear-engined, air-cooled VWs could co-exist. (URO Automotive)

trend continuing with modern small cars, where they appear to do well when put through artificial safety tests in isolation. However, they tend to do less well when weight is incorporated into the test. To show the trade off in safety when downsizing from a larger, heavier compact sized car like the VW 412 to a subcompact like the Golf or Passat, the NHTSA and Calspan did an offset crash test between an AMC Concord two-door sedan and two-door VW Rabbit in 1980. Both vehicles were traveling at 32mph. The compact Concord's survival cell remained intact, and driver/passenger crash test dummies recorded low HIC (head injury criteria) of 160/180.

The VW Rabbit's respective HIC 630/365 readings were higher, but

consistent with survival. More worrying was the degree of passenger cell deformation and dashboard intrusion. These occurrences would likely have resulted in a trapped driver, with lower body injuries. VW had completed a new Engineering and Safety Center by the early '70s. The Safety Center employed 700 people, with most of the test equipment and crash test dummies coming from America. In addition, VW had also been tenuously involved with the US ESV program. However, then as now, it seems a smaller, lighter vehicle is unable to protect its occupants as well as a heavier vehicle. The German ADAC's replication of the test using an Audi Q7 and Fiat 500 proves the point.

Fortunately for VW and its rivals,

safety didn't sell in the 1970s or 1980s. The new VWs had the right stats, where it counted for consumers. Rudolf Leiding was also watching the pennies in VW's transition to a front-drive, water-cooled future. That is, making the most of current inventory. The new Scirocco used the same knob as the Beetle for its seatback release. Then there was project EA425. This was the new Audi badged coupe that was Porsche designed, and would utilize many unglamorous parts from the VW Group's parts shelf. VW knew about the planned Porsche 928, and Leiding initiated EA425 to add diversity and pizzazz to the VW Group while using humble parts wherever possible. Indeed, the North American Beetle's continued usage of four-wheel drum brakes, when Euro versions had been harnessing front disks for years, seemed a fine way to run down parts stockpiles.

With the model transition under way, a Beetle replacement located, and new conventional ideas in the offing, VW seemed to have turned the corner. Rudolf Leiding saw blue skies over Wolfsburg for 1974. Unfortunately, the fuel crisis and ensuing recession, made the bad times stretch. In 1972-73 VW was making less profit, but was still in the black. In 1974 it made its first loss, and even the presence of Passat, Scirocco and Golf weren't enough. It was bad timing for Leiding. When other proposals he had weren't accepted by management, he was forced to move on.

In January 1975 Rudolf Leiding resigned, and in February Toni Schmuecker became the new chairman. He was formerly with Ford Germany, and had success in the troubled German steel industry. By August 1975 VW was back in profit due to three reasons: economizing, job cuts

and a subsidence of the recession. As part of the slash and burn, Toni Schmuecker cancelled EA425. VW already had the Scirocco, so EA425 was an unnecessary extravagance. In addition, he sold Porsche's work back to Porsche, and put Zuffenhausen on a contract leading to 1979. Here, Porsche would buy VW parts to build the entry level Porsche 924.

The Porsche 924 was a great way to use up Beetle and Golf parts. Better still, for a few more Deutschmarks VW Group would even build the 924 for Porsche! The NSU Neckarsulm werks would be the 924's home. Toni Schmuecker also made the decision, that 1976 would be the VW Beetle 1303's last year. However, the most important of his measures, were job cuts. In his words, "A couple of months after I came, we actually had difficulty meeting the payrolls." He added, "We were making cars not according to market demand but according to the number of workers we had. We were sinking."[16]

Pipe-smoking Schmuecker had the knack of working with unions, and he took actions similar to those Lee Iacocca would take at Chrysler in 1979. In a word, the answer was downsizing. Rabbit or no, it was slash and burn 'til you earn, and the unions weren't buying it. CEO Toni Schmuecker cut 20% of the workforce in 1975-76. The redundancy payout averaged four grand per person. Older workers were encouraged to take early retirement, working wives to give up, and guest workers to go home. As Chrysler Corp. would do, even with new front-drive models, VW had to adjust from the company it was, to the company it would become in the 1980s and 1990s. It used to be a world player, now it would be just a major European force.

Even in such difficult times,

Volkswagen Volkswagenwerk AG, Postfach, D-3180 Wolfsburg, Deutschland

Als letztes Überbleibsel der Nachkriegsgeneration steht nur noch der Mexiko-Käfer im Programm. Das heißgeliebte Käfer-Cabrio mußte nun auch dem Zug der Zeit weichen und dem Golf-Cabrio Platz machen. Nostalgie hin oder her — Tatsache bleibt, daß VW mit seinen wassergekühlten Fronttrieblern seit Jahren enorme Gewinne erzielt. Gewaltige Investitionen sollen die Position im In- und Ausland weiter stärken.

VW Käfer
Der Käfer lebt nach wie vor,

besonders in der dritten Welt, aber auch noch hierzulande. Seit gut einem Jahr kommt er aus Mexiko als Einheitsmodell reinsten Wassers zu uns: nur 34 PS-Motor und L-Ausstattung, keine Extras ab Werk.

VW Polo/Derby
Der Polo, Zweitürer mit Heckklappe, lief 1975 vom Stapel. Frontmotor quer eingebaut. Anfang 1977 erhielt er einen Bruder mit größerem Gepäckraum im Stufenheck — den Popo-Polo. Beide Varianten sind technisch völlig identisch.

VW 1200 L — 25 kW, 115 km/h

 VW Polo — 29–44 kW, 135–154 km/h

 VW Derby — 29–44 kW, 135–154 km/h

VW Golf — 37–51 kW, 140–153 km/h | VW Golf GTI — 81 kW, 182 km/h

 VW Golf Cabriolet — 51–81 kW, 155–180 km/h

After 1978, European buyers could still get a new Beetle. However, it now came from Mexico. This official VW import arrangement continued into 1985. (Courtesy Vereinigte Motor-Verlage)

the West German workforce was cooperative. There was a spirit of Mitbestimmung, or co-determination. Workers' representatives were on the supervisory boards of large West German corporations. It explained the lower incidence of industrial action in this country, compared to more socialist 1970s nations like Britain and France. In the first half of 1976, days lost to strike action per 1000 workers was 19 in West Germany, but 70 in Britain and 177 in France.

In spite of such relative labor relations harmony, Schmuecker's austerity measures were difficult to swallow. Workers had one third

of the supervisory board vote, but owners had the majority. Workers opposed the job cuts at VW, but the owners had the final say. It was the first non-unanimous vote in VW corporate history. However, there was no subsequent strike, and unions co-operated with the aforementioned austerity measures. In many ways it was reality bites at VW, with the fuel crisis having thrown such an almighty curveball. 1973 had been a bumper sales year for the North American market, and although VW wasn't a big winner that year, it had added 12,200 workers at this time. Similarly, the VW tech boys had been working on a stratified charge Wankel rotary engine in the early '70s. The fuel crisis made all this, and the Audi/Porsche 924, pure extravagance.

With Toni Schmuecker VW found the stability it needed. He remained CEO until 1982, when Carl Hahn took over for 1982-83. Hahn was a long time VW stalwart, and a big part of VWoA's rise to prominence during the 1960s. By now the VW Quantumn/Santana, a Dasher/Passat with conventional trunk, was made in Japan on VW's behalf by Nissan. At this time, Nissan also hooked up with Alfa Romeo, to build the Alfa-badged Nissan Cherry in Italy as the Alfa Arna. Then there was the Nissan plant in Sunderland, UK and the Smyrna plant Stateside. It was all about getting around trade barriers.

WAITING FOR GOLF
VW liked to advertise in the UK that their Golf was the number one import in Japan. However, VW made a smaller impact in Japan than Japanese automakers made in VW's once crucial market of North America. If the Beetle had been overtaken by fancy Datsun and Toyota imports in America, then surely the new Rabbit (VW Golf) would

redress the balance of power? The new Golf got VW back on track, but it was a qualified success. The situation was shown at the summer 1975 Silverstone Annual Michelin International Test Car Show. The event was covered by UK TV's *Drive In* car show, looking at the reasons so many Continental and Japanese cars were selling in Britain. Among the top ten imported cars was the new VW Golf, introduced in this market late in 1974.

Drive In presenter Tony Bastable asked *London Evening News* motoring correspondent Sue Barker why the Continental and Japanese brands had proved so popular. Space efficiency and fold-down rear seats that went with the hatchback format were the main reasons given. A competitive specification in design and standard equipment for the price were also stated. Better build quality and reliability were reasons skirted around. These facets seemed more applicable to the Japanese Toyota and Datsun, than the French Renaults or Fiat 127. Of the Japanese cars shown, the Toyota Crown, Datsun Bluebird, Cherry and Sunny, only the Cherry

was a front-driver available with hatchback.

The Japanese contingent consisted of mostly very conventional rear-drive sedans. Two things were ominous: Datsun alone had grabbed nearly 5% of the British market, and the green VW Golf on display had a badly misaligned bumper. Bastable introduced the Golf as a Beetle successor, but its quality didn't seem familiar to VW traditionalists. However, for Britain and Europe it seemed the Golf had enough quality, and that its good design and efficiency would carry this and other new generation VWs high in the European sales charts. That said, for buyers that focused on reliability, equipment and price, the Japanese companies were very competitive, especially in North America.

Fiat Boss Vittorio Ghidella said in the 1980s, "The Japanese operate particularly in relation to the American market: they produce essentially small American cars, not really small European ones."[17] An accurate observation perhaps, but worrying for VW, since North America was a very key market for Wolfsburg. Evidence

The commercially crucial VW Golf was introduced in the wake of the fuel crisis. This 1976 Elektro Golf was an all-electric study into alternative fuels. (Courtesy Volkswagen AG)

that the new VWs were not up to Beetle quality standards was apparent in testing by independent journals. For example, in July 1975 *Consumer Reports* examined the new AMC Pacer and VW Rabbit. The Pacer was delivered with 17 defects, but the Rabbit (Golf) came with 34!

Consumer Reports, a puritanical ally of VW for decades, appreciated the Rabbit's design efficiency, but this came at a price. The 3.8-liter six-cylinder Pacer, with automatic transmission and power steering was $3973, while the stick shift 1.5-liter Rabbit was $4015. In addition, the Rabbit had a mere 12-month, 12,000 mile warranty, or half what the immortal Bug offered. Some of this gulf was due to the strong Deutschmark.[18] Indeed, during 1975 the Rabbit's price rose by a tremendous $350 due to the exchange rate appreciation.

Pricing aside, VW was introducing a complete new range of cars that shared no major components with the previous air-cooled models. Even at the best of times new models have teething problems. In this case it was a new Passat, Scirocco, Golf and Polo, and VW didn't have the luxury of time anymore. Ideally the Rabbit should have been ready for '73 MY, not '75 MY. That would have given VW some chance of holding on to the North American economy car market. However, the new VWs weren't inexpensive, even laying aside the exchange rate issue, and the development of the Golf/Rabbit was carried out at warp speed, because, in the words of *Road & Track* publisher John R Bond, VW fiddled while Rome burned.

When interviewed on the Golf's silver anniversary, Giorgetto Giugiaro said VW management, in trying to replace the Beetle, were, "No, not nervous, but they were in a hurry." Originally brought on board to do a concept car, Giugiaro was now designing VW's great Wolfsburg hope. At first the Italian designer wanted square headlamps, one of the few VW interferences was to request round lights. Most likely this was to fit in with American lighting laws, which showed VW hadn't given up on America, yet. Giugiaro and his firm ItalDesign had done some of the most exotic and beautiful cars in the world. He was asked why then was he now doing an econobox? His response was, "I have to eat!" The Wolfsburg volks also told Giugiaro of design requirements in relation to Passat, not Beetle. It truly was a new VW era.[19]

Giugiaro and VW had to put food on the table. However, in the speedy drive to introduce all new cars, with new hardware, an old German saying was forgotten. That is, you must not slaughter the cow if you want to milk it. Quality on the 1975 Rabbit wasn't up to VW standards, and proved a real surprise to magazine testers and VW devotees alike. *Road & Track* had a gasoline Rabbit 1500 on long-term test. Their experience wasn't good and in May 1976 stated, "People have traditionally bought VWs because they are inexpensive to buy, have an excellent reliability record and a service and parts supply that is supreme. Having bought a VW for $4729 and then to be confronted with a bill for $600 and a delay for parts of five weeks on a nine-month-old car is disappointing to say the least."

Road & Track experienced the hardship of being in car trouble, and out of warranty. They found the automaker would only help, "... if you bitch loud and long enough ..." Problems included a dash rattle, poorly installed radio, rubber doughnut exhaust hangers that failed every 5000 miles, and a faulty rear window defogger. *R&T*'s mishaps were hardly atypical, many other buyers had plenty of trouble too. Something had to be done, and was. In 1976 VWoA did a recall program for Rabbits, Sciroccos and Dashers. There were engine tune adjustments, parts upgrades, and trim replacement to largely bring the earlier troubled cars up to improved '76 MY spec.

The 1976 front-drive VWs were much better, the way they should have been from the start. If only Wolfsburg had more time. The latest 1.6-liter cars had less NVH issues, fewer problems, and seemed more durable. The interiors had resembled something from an austerity rally, now they were plusher. Still not up to Super Beetle La Grande Bug standards though. Indeed, the mechanical and trim foibles of the new Rabbit would have saddened the hearts of air-cooled faithful. To think the VW 412 had to make way for this recalled Rabbit.

Automotive scribes couldn't hide their euphoria over how well the Rabbit drove. The same critics that had panned the air-cooled brigade since the mid-'60s. However, the Beetle was still going in 1975/76 America. Its Bosch L-jetronic fuel-injection, and high quality contrasted with carb fed Rabbits, and their drivability woes. Improvements or no, many buyers continued with, or turned to, Toyota Corollas, Datsun 210s (Sunny) and Dodge Colts (Mitsubishi). In Britain VW tried to avoid direct price competition with the Japanese contingent, so too in America. However, here the upscale Honda Civic and Accords cost more than plainer Japanese brands, and met the Rabbit head on with quality and an extensive standard equipment list.

WESTMORELAND VWS – MADE IN AMERICA!

Even a premium econocar has to be price competitive. Making cars in America would help VW overcome that ol' currency monkey on the back. Building VWs Stateside had been a long time in the thinking. Now it was a reality and a necessity. VW's worker's representatives voted in favor of a US plant. President of the West German Metalworkers' Union, Eugen Loderer, said it should have been done 10 years earlier. As a VW supervisory board

This Westmoreland-built, fuel-sipping Rabbit pickup helped VWoA rebound to 3% market share, in the wake of the second world fuel crisis of 1979/80. (Courtesy Syme Magazines)

member, Loderer was pro the USA factory, but with conditions. American VW production would only be sold in the US and Canada. Plus, production increases would require supervisory board approval.

So it was that VW became the first foreign automaker after WWII, to make cars in America. In October 1976 a former Chrysler plant was bought, with production of Rabbits commencing in April 1978. The place was Westmoreland, Pennsylvania, and VW Jettas would eventually be made there too. Unlike later Japanese, German and Korean automakers hanging out their shingle in America in the 1980s and 1990s, Westmoreland was a UAW (United Auto Workers) union workforce factory. While it would be inaccurate to say Westmoreland was to Rabbit what Lordstown was to Vega … they weren't exactly making Fabergé eggs there.

Worldwide, it took the Golf 31 months to reach its first million. Westmoreland had a lot of production capacity, an ability to turn out 200,000 units per annum. VWoA also had great expectations, with an aim of 5% of the North American market. For years there had been a patriotic sentiment in America, not happy with the concept of imports taking jobs from Detroit. Now the Rabbit was as American as mom's apple pie, or failing that, strudel. In contrast, Rabbit's very popular opposition wasn't made in the USA. In 1982 PBS TV show *MotorWeek* took a gander at the new pilgrim's progress. Host John H Davis introduced a whole show devoted to an 'Econobox Comparison.'

In the wake of the second gas crunch, four-cylinder small cars were increasingly king of the formerly American V8 corral. So had project Rabbit worked? Five years on had it been able to reclaim the Beetle's once 'numero uno' econocar position, and wrestle market share away from the Japanese? On test were the Dodge Colt, Renault Le Car, Nissan Sentra and ye olde Rabbit. The Colt was a captive import from Mitsubishi. It had become the North American subcompact gold standard. It was the little car that acted like a big car.

Just as in years gone by, with the Big Three studying the Beetle, the now Worried Three were taking Colts apart, to see what made them tick. The Le Car was made in France since 1972, but was sold through AMC dealers. AMC was by this stage largely Renault owned and controlled. The Le Car (Renault 5) was promoted as the world's most popular front-driver. Globally this was true, and worrying to VW. Renault was duking it out with VW in Europe, yes they made front-drive hatchbacks too. Even worse, Renault was going to make the Renault 9 in Kenosha for '83 MY. All handy for driving to the store, to pick up an Atari 5200 and discounted ET game cartridge! Le Regie had grand designs on North America. The Le Car was a mere aperitif.

Then there was the new Nissan Sentra. For years the rear-drive Datsun 210 (Sunny) had wowed them in the sales charts, and with primo gas mileage. Now they were called Nissans and came with front-drive, but were still made in Japan. Fiat's boss Vittorio Ghidella was right about Japanese automakers being much more simpatico with the US market. The Sentra was big, for a small car. It had a conventional trunk and a soft wallowy ride, all for fuel sipping in comfort over endless miles of gray interstate. So one would be well rested when seeing Aunt Patti for the holidays.

The Rabbit had also made concessions to the American market. *Road & Track* even described the 1976 interiors of Rabbit and Dasher, as Americanized. With the 1982 Rabbit *MotorWeek* found great brakes, but ride comfort had been given a higher priority than handling. That said, the staff found this Pennsylvanian built VW to be well put together, and possessing good paint. Playing against stereotypes, the Renault Le Car was also well made. So too the Dodge Colt, but the Sentra displayed surprising quality lapses for a Japanese car. Perhaps teething problems for the new Sentra/Sunny? Homer Simpson was once asked by a young lady, if he would like to try some free chocolate chip cookies? He did, and when asked how they were, he replied, "Well, the price is right." In *MotorWeek*'s test the Rabbit was the only test vehicle made in America, and it was also the most expensive. In a similar vein Renault started making cars in America in 1983, care of American Motors. Kenosha's newest Caddy, the Alliance, sold very well in the hundreds of thousands. Like the VW Golf/Rabbit it was critically praised, winning the 1982 European Car of the Year title.

Road & Track, Car and Driver et al agreed. They said 'vive la difference,' and that the Alliance had a driver's car edge on the Japanese. From '84 MY there was even the hatchback Encore version (Renault 11). So what went wrong? Apart from many cases of component and poor assembly quality, the labor cost issue was a big one. Production, using a UAW workforce, had to be very high before a profit could be turned. In 1986 a South Korean autoworker got paid one sixth the level of his UAW counterpart. So making a small car in America was like having your good arm tied behind your back in an arm wrestling contest.

VW set up shop in America to overcome exchange rate cost issues,

A late model Mk1 Golf GTi at a 2016 Wourthesee VW meet. The iconic Golf GTi heralded a new high glamor image for Wolfsburg. (Courtesy Susanne Wiersch)

but the labor cost Stateside largely undid their plans. In 1986 the world price of oil collapsed, and took with it most of the American econocar market. So Renault's plans for US domination went the way of Napoleon. The small car market shrunk back so that it only supported the Japanese, and now Korean Hyundais. It was really game over for VWoA's Westmoreland built Golfs and Jettas. The factory had switched to Golf 2 in 1984, with the Jetta continuing alongside until March 1988.

The Westmoreland factory made 1.15 million cars to the end of 1988 model year. The good times peaked at 3% US market share in 1980, in the wake of the second fuel crisis. A time when US buyers were going econocar and diesel crazy. Naturally, the Rabbit Diesel combined both elements in the one package. However, according to John Holusha of the *New York Times*, market share fell to 1.9% by late 1987. The plant was only making 60,000 cars per annum by this stage.[20] Even though the iconic Rabbit GTi was introduced in 1983, and Golf 2 thereafter,

The Golf continues to be commercially important for VW. Here, Hidemi Aoki is with her 2014 VW Golf Mk7. (Courtesy www. nepoeht.com)

ESCAPE FROM DETROIT

The truth was that VW ran into the same problem Detroit did earlier. It's hard to profitably make a small car in America using unionized workers. There were three ways around this, concerning the 'beer can on four-wheels' market. One, import a small car from a low cost country – the '87 MY Hyundai Excel hatchback was $4995 and sold 264,000 copies in America. Two, the backdoor import variation – the Ford Festiva was a Mazda 121, made in Korea by Kia. Solution number three, make your small car on a non-UAW greenfield site, and take advantage of a state's financial generosity to set up a factory in an area of high unemployment. GM eventually took option three, with the Saturn plant in Tennessee. However, the Japanese did that trick first, with the Nissan Sentra at Smyrna.

By the close of VW Golf production at Westmoreland, the cheapest Golf was $7990. VW was competing with 35 brands, many of which undercut its prices handsomely. The loss of the American car market by German makes, largely VW, can be seen from figures between 1970 and 1982. The Japanese annual market share for 1970, 1973, 1976,1979 and 1982, were a respective 3.7%, 6.5%, 9.3%, 16.6% and 22.6%. West Germany's market share for the same years were 8.9%, 6.9%, 3.7%, 3.3% and 3.1%. By 1976 VWoA had switched to the Rabbit as their volume selling model.

The figures show that in America the Rabbit was unable to replace the Beetle as a high volume selling small car. They also show that producing cars in America didn't restore VW's former competitiveness in this market.[21] 1983 statistics also reveal that while Europe was exporting 420,000 cars to America, Japan was

Westmoreland didn't turn a profit in its final five years. If success has many fathers, failure has even more critics. Industry commentators said VW hadn't followed up on Beetle, therefore letting the Japanese snare the honey pot. The UAW blamed VW management for not offering a sufficiently appealing product to the public to safeguard its members' jobs.

sending 1.86 million. This was right on the quota limit, and explained why Japanese and Korean automakers got into making cars in America. Make two cars Stateside, and you get to import one over and above existing limits.

Back in Europe the Golf had done well from day one. It was the number one selling car in Germany for 17 years, all the way through Golf Mk1 and Mk2.[22] This was what mattered to VW at the time for two reasons. One, it made the company profitable. Secondly, with the general European exodus from America, the new game was to be number one in Europe. In the mid-'80s Fiat's boss Vittorio Ghidella said (as if 'Fix It Again Tony' really had a choice?) that they were glad to be out of America. Renault sold out its AMC interest to Chrysler by the late '80s. Peugeot was also out of actively selling cars in North America by the early '90s.

Apart from British-made Japanese cars, where the Peugeot/Citroën PSA boss referred to Britain as a Japanese aircraft carrier, the European automakers slugged and discounted it out on home turf. By 1992 VW was number one in Europe again. A decade earlier, it had been Renault. However, now VW was the one to watch. It was now free to 'high-tech' itself into the future.

THE FUEL OF THE FUTURE
Even prior to the fuel crisis, VW was studying alternative vehicle fuel strategies. There was an electric Type 2 Bus, with batteries that lived between the axles, and under the bed locker. It seemed well suited to the short-range, urban commercial use. VW was working with West Germany's largest producer of electricity Rheinisch-Westfalische Elektrizitatswerk AG. Rapid charge batteries and special

charge stations were part of the plan. After the fuel crisis, work in this area continued. The 1976 Elektro-Golf was a Rabbit that was converted to electric power as part of VW's alternative energy study. However, a lack of infrastructure and limited buyer interest, even in green movement dominated 21st Century Germany, has seen modest sales from the modern all electric Golf. Such universal electric car adoption, remain the utopian dreams of lobby groups, politicians and bureaucrats.

VW's gas turbine Type 2 Bus had 70bhp and two rotary heat exchangers, from Williams Research of Michigan. A hope from the pre-gas crunch days, gas turbine vehicles were noisy and thirsty. The experimental Bus only got 15mpg, and produced high levels of nitrogen oxides. It proved another dead end. Many automakers were into compartmentalized combustion chambers, the stratified charge engine. Most of the chamber was lean, a small part was rich. The rich part ignited the lean segment, making good power with a clean tailpipe. VW did one of these in air-cooled flat-four form, with computer controlled fuel-injection.

Stratified charge was a winner early on, with CVCC Civics, Accords and Preludes lighting the way. However, they couldn't solely cope with stricter pollution laws. VW's stratified charge Wankel engine fell foul of durability problems, and thirst, in the wake of the first fuel crisis. Out of all the project trying, the best bet seemed to be diesel. A long used commercial vehicle method, but for passenger cars? It was timely indeed that in 1973, on the eve of the gas crunch, VW management gave the go ahead to do 1½ ton diesel trucks. This proved valuable preparation for converting the Dasher's 1500 motor to a diesel diet.

So there it was on the VW proving grounds of Ehra-Lessien, a 50mpg VW Golf in 1976. It met all current federal pollution laws, sans smog controls. *Road & Track*'s Jan P Norbye said, "If you're worried about smoke and odor, forget it." In 1977 the Golf Diesel became the world's first mass produced diesel small car. With a July 1977 *R&T* test showing 0-60mph in 15.8 seconds, 43mpg and 90mph in 4th, it seemed like the future had arrived.

With environmentalists and scientists claiming the world was going to run out of oil by 1987, the Golf Diesel seemed the perfect car to drive into the apocalypse. Jane Fonda's TV reporter character virtuously drove a Rabbit Diesel in 1979's *The China Syndrome* movie. The stats were great, but compared to the smoothness of the VW Type 4's flat-four, that diesel 1500 had the audible charm of a spoon dropped into a kitchen waste disposal unit. There were also practical concerns.

If you weren't 18-wheeler truckers like BJ McKay and the Bear, diesel could be hard to find. *Road & Track*'s editor fought through traffic in the magazine's long-term test, non-a/c Rabbit Diesel, trying to reach the one local gas station with diesel. He was then greeted with the sign "No Diesel Today." To this he said, "I wouldn't have an effing diesel if you paid me to take it away. And you can quote me."

Still, in spite of such travails, and unexpected repair costs, the *R&T* Rabbit Diesel made dollars and sense. Due to rampant inflation and fuel crisis diesel popularity, *Road & Track*'s 3½-year-old Rabbit Diesel was worth nearly the same as the new 1977 model! However, a further ominous caveat was that while early Rabbit Diesels could easily pass current smog tests, they would have trouble meeting

The expanding VW Group now includes Audi, Bentley and Porsche. Hidemi Aoki poses with the 2018 Audi RS3. (Courtesy www.nepoeht. com)

proposed nitrogen oxide limits beyond 1981.

EPILOG – GOING FOR GOLD – NO 1 IN THE WORLD

In the 1990s and 2000s improvements in turbodiesel technology, and European government's continued exorbitant fuel excise, made diesel cars the default choice for that continent's buyers. In the mainstream market VW Group was very good with diesel tech, cementing its dominance in Europe. With subsequent historical developments, VW Group would get a shot at being Number One in the world, not just Europe. This it achieved in 2016 and 2017.

After the Global Financial Crisis, an ailing GM sought a taxpayer handout, and tried to produce more in China. Ford would try to move production to Mexico. Of course, VW also expanded car production in both China and Mexico. Producing in China, and for China, makes money. Renault and Fiat would go on to vicariously enjoy the North American car market, through Nissan and Chrysler respectively. It all left Toyota and VW to battle it out for the master of the universe title.

When VW's Westmoreland plant was winding down in 1987, it got the Brazilian-built subcompact Fox, backdoor imported for American sale. The UAW feared this act would become more common, and they were right. It was your choice of a Mexican-made Golf, or greenfield-built Camry. Still, even giants slip on banana skins.

With Toyota there were the 'floormats of death,' that allegedly caused their cars to accelerate out of control. Then there was VW's Dieselgate revelations. In both cases the public got over it. Toyota drivers drove without floormats until new safety mats could be designed. In VW's case the state of California eventually cleared existing diesel stock for sale, whereupon buyers swooped in to get a discounted diesel. Which just goes to show no one lets the environment get in the way of a good deal.

VW Group has grown to include such diverse members as Bentley, Porsche and Skoda. Using the versatile MQB platform, economies of scale can be achieved across a number of mainstream and prestige model lines. If there is some disappointment, it comes from the retro Beetle's 2019 demise. Come 2020 it will be the first year without a brand new Beetle of some kind since 1937. In all that has happened, and may yet happen, one thing is certain. VW has come a long way from the Bug!

*By 2016-2017, Wolfsburg was everyone's mug of Joe **and** cup of tea. In spite of Dieselgate, VW was the largest automaker on the planet. (Courtesy Mike)*

APPENDIX A
SPECIFICATION TABLES

1969 411 COUPE FOUR-SPEED

List price	7700DM
Engine	OHV all aluminum case Type 4 EA flat-four motor, 90mm x 66mm, 1679cc (102.5ci), 68bhp @ 4500rpm, 91lb/ft @ 2800rpm, 7.8:1 CR, 2 x Solex 34 PDSIT carburetors
Dimensions	179.2in length, 64.3in width, 58.4in height
Weight	2380lb
Luggage capacity	400 liters (frunk)
Front/rear track	54.2in/52.8in
Gearbox	Four-speed manual transaxle – 3.81 (1st), 2.11 (2nd), 1.40 (3rd), 1.00 (4th), 3.73:1 (final drive ratio)
Front suspension	MacPherson struts, lower control arms, coil springs, tube shocks, anti swaybar
Rear suspension	Semi-trailing arms, coil springs, tube shocks
Wheels and tires	15x4.5in steel rims and 155-15in radials
Brakes	11.1in solid disk (front), 9.8in x 1.78in drum (rear). Swept area 311in^2
0-100km/h	17.4 seconds
Top speed	147km/h
Fuel economy	12.2 liters per 100km

PERFORMANCE/ECONOMY DATA:
RAINER GUENZLER AUTOTESTS NO 135 VW 411
The Type 4 made its debut in Europe as a 1969 carburetor model. It was the largest car VW had released at that point in time, and the first with a unibody and four-door availability. It was pricey, but came with a lot of standard equipment, and a big 'frunk!'

1971 411E FOUR-DOOR SEDAN AUTOMATIC

List price	$3074
Engine	OHV all aluminum case Type 4 EA flat-four motor, 90mm x 66mm, 1679cc (102.5ci), 80bhp @ 4900rpm, 97lb/ft @ 2700rpm, 8.2:1 CR, Bosch D-jetronic fuel-injection
Dimensions	179.2in length, 64.3in width, 58.4in height
Weight	2430lb
Luggage capacity	8.1ft^3 (frunk) 2.2ft^3 (rear seat well)
Front/rear track	54.1in/53in
Gearbox	Three-speed VW/Borg Warner 003 automatic – 2.65 (1st), 1.59 (2nd), 1.00 (3rd), 3.67:1 (final drive ratio)
Front suspension	MacPherson struts, lower control arms, coil springs, tube shocks, anti swaybar
Rear suspension	Semi-trailing arms, coil springs, tube shocks
Wheels and tires	15x4.5in steel rims and 155-15in radials
Brakes	11.1in solid disk (front), 9.8in x 1.78in drum (rear). Swept area 311in^2
0-60mph	16.3 seconds
Top speed	84mph
Fuel economy	22.5mpg (US gallon)

PERFORMANCE/ECONOMY DATA:
***ROAD & TRACK* FEBRUARY 1971**

The Type 4 made a very late North American market entry … April 1971! Four-door sedans and Variants came with automatic transmission as standard. Even so, 117,110 were sold, and as *Car and Track*'s Bud Lindemann said, "Then, too, at least now a Beetle owner has something to graduate to."

APPENDIX B
SPORTING VWs

VW KARMANN GHIA

With VWs becoming more popular by the minute in the 1950s, thoughts turned to the glamor angle. The idea of a sporty VW based on the humble Bug platform, and mechanicals, came from Dr Wilhelm Karmann. The Osnabruck coachbuilder sought design aid from Ghia's Luigi Serge.[23] VW flipped over the idea after seeing the prototype, and a legend started in October 1955. The Karmann Ghia's front section, was composed of three separate panels. Production proved to be a high-quality, labor-intensive affair of low volume.

The Karmann Ghia was priced way under the Porsche 356, but was always an image bridge between

This '71 Karmann Ghia convertible combined Beetle reliability with sporting good looks. (Courtesy Patrick Baptist)

Wolfsburg and Zuffenhausen, by way of Osnabruck. You may have never won a race in a stock Karmann Ghia, but that wasn't the point. Between 1962 and 1969 a Type 3 Karmann Ghia was already offered, with razor edge styling courtesy of Sergio Sartorelli. Unlike the Type 1 based Karmann Ghia, the razor edge model was only available in coupe form, and only in Europe. The Type 1 Karmann Ghia coupe and ragtop ran to 364,401 and 80,899 respectively. The Type 3 edition accounted for 42,498 units. The grand total was 487,798, and that's a lot of style!

VW SP-2

A truly sporty VW was created by VW do Brasil. By July 1970 the one millionth VW had rolled off the line at the Sao Paolo works. VW do Brasil had over 50% of the market, and locally designed four-door Type 3 1600s. With time on their hands, the VW subsidiary's designers worked on sports car Project X, under former Brasil VEMAG (DKW) boss Wilhelm Schmiemann. They targeted the fellow that was into the VW aftermarket performance scene. VW do Brasil boss Rudolf Leiding encouraged the project, and green lighted it prior to his return to West Germany to run Audi.

Named after where it was made, the VW SP-2 made a March 1971 debut at the Sao Paolo German Trade Show. The coupe was very well received, and went on sale in June 1972. Utilizing the full length Type 3 platform, long stroke Type 3 motor and traditional torsion bar front, swing axle rear suspension, the SP-2 was Beetle reliable under that very jazzy body. The 1678cc motor

Like the VW 412, the Type 1-based Karmann Ghia lived on through 1974, and represented traditional air-cooled Volkswagen. (Courtesy Patrick Baptist)

The VW SP-2 was a Type 3-based, rear-engined sports car. It was a creation of VW do Brasil, when that subsidiary was under future VW CEO Rudolf Leiding. (Courtesy Dr Aiken Brent Krahmer)

By using the Type 3 platform, the SP-2 was a roomy two-seater with ample luggage storage, fore and aft. It was a low-slung 45.6 in high, also! (Courtesy Dr Aiken Brent Krahmer)

had big 39mm intake valves, plus a big cam. However, the 7.5:1 compression ratio, necessary for low octane Brazilian gas, limited power to 65bhp. That said, Brazil had a vast 'hop up' aftermarket for VW flat fours.

The sheer speed of Project X, meant the export legality of the SP-2's low set headlamps were overlooked. Even so, of the 10,193 coupes made up to December 1975, 681 were indeed exported. The biggest destination was Nigeria with 155 cars, next was Kuwait with 90 units. That said, two made it to America during model currency. One car each made it to South Africa, Angola, Portugal, Iraq and Iran. Inside, fresh air dash vents complemented the jacaranda trimmed shifter, handbrake and heater controls. The driving experience was traditional air-cooled VW, solid, insulated and smooth. Handling limits were low on stock rubber, but the progression to oversteer was gradual. Overall, the VW SP-2 was very likeable, with an easy shift four-speed.[24]

BRADLEY GT

Do you want a frugal sports car? Do you want the looks of Corvette and VW dependability, in the one car? Well, Gary Bradley thought you did. The trouble was, Gary Bradley didn't

exist … confused? Following in the rich tradition of Porsche, Denzel, Apal and even the Brazilian Puma, Bradley Automotive offered its GT from 1970. Salesman extraordinaire Gary Courneya and designer David Bradley Fuller were involved with Gary's Bug Shop in the late '60s. This operation made dune buggy kits. Following on from the Bug Shop, was Bradley Automotive. The latter's GT was a simple, fiberglass-bodied sports car based on a Beetle platform and mechanicals.

The early torsion bar front swing-axle rear suspension was utilized. The two-seater T-top body had hinged gullwing plastic side panels, covers over the headlamps and a C2 Vette windshield. One could buy a kit, or have it ready made, even aftermarket

With a 65bhp Type 1 1700, the VW SP-2 did 0-60mph in 16 seconds and almost 100mph. Almost 30mpg on low octane Brazilian gas was pretty good, too.
In the words of the VW SP-2 brochure: "Its advanced design may be compared with the boldness of your ideas. Its elegance will harmonize with the charm of your companion. You see that the SP-2 was made for two people. Uncommon people. You and your companion." (Courtesy Dr Aiken Brent Krahmer)

Like Ferry Porsche, fellow Austrian Wolfgang Denzel utilized VW Beetle hardware to create a 1950s sports car. (Author)

Bradley Automotive wasn't really affiliated with the Thor Corporation. However, at least by 1976, the Bradley GT and its brochure existed! (Courtesy SunRay Products)

a/c was available. Gary Courneya was a kind of go-getter. The project was facilitated by one major backer, and crowd-funding. In those halcyon times, a widely disseminated Bradley GT flyer was circulated. Send one buck for a brochure, it said. Trouble was, when the scheme started, the brochure, and even the car, didn't exist! However, trusting souls as did exist back then, the one dollar payments did indeed substantially bankroll said project. More than this, Courneya even took to telephoning prospects in the guise of the fictitious Gary Bradley!

Courneya probably wanted Gary Bradley to be the Ronald McDonald of cars, and by the early '70s, he was. By the mid '70s Bradley Automotive was a successful business, with around 6000 GTs made. The company then invested one million dollars to create an upscale sports car. This was the more refined and sophisticated Bradley GT II. Designed by John Chan, the GT II had

One celebrity Bradley GT owner was Liberace. The entertainer had his VW-based sports car custom painted in metallic gold flake. (Courtesy Binksternet)

real gullwing doors, electric pop ups and VDO jet cockpit gauges as part of the upgrades. However, the Bradley Automotive business took a nose dive. Staff defected to rival Fiber Fab, kits/parts and franchises were promised, but not realized. Indeed, the Minnesota attorney general brought up even more fraudulent business practices.

Bradley Automotive traded under Chapter 11 bankruptcy until April 1980. At this point, in the wake of the second fuel crisis, the firm launched an electric powered version of its GT II. Fifty GTEs were done. The company finally went belly up in 1981. Celebrity Bradley GT owners included pianist Liberace and tennis player Andrea Jaeger. Presidential candidate Barry Goldwater had a GT II. Other VW based kit specials included the Scorpion GT and Lithia GT. All from the era when Type 1 Beetles dominated the North American roadscape, providing a reliable and affordable sports car basis.

THE SQUARE PORSCHE

With the April 1 1969 VW-Porsche VG GmbH joint venture, Wolfsburg and Porsche seemed to have the perfect sports car to serve their purposes. The VW-Porsche 914 was closer to Porsche than the Karmann Ghia, and would be a more cost-effective entry level Porsche than the 912. However, things didn't quite go to plan with the Osnabruck mid-engined two-seater, built largely by Karmann. Ferry Porsche had a gentleman's agreement, with long time VW boss and friend Heinz Nordhoff, concerning the price of 914 bodies. After Nordhoff's death, new VW CEO Dr Kurt Lotz wanted a higher price.

The 914 had to contend with a relatively expensive price tag, strong Deutschmark, and competition from the Opel GT, Datsun 240Z and Ford/

If you're going to build a machine, build the best!
The Amante GT

Style . . . performance . . . engineering . . . all put together in a stack of dynamite called The Amante GT. The fiberglas body with a list of exclusive quality features as long as Le Mans:

☐ steel tubing side rails and roll bar laminated between the uni-shell body and innerliner. Doors structured on tubing framework. ☐ mechanically operated pop-away headlight covers ☐ hard polyester finish that needs no painting ☐ inner-lined passenger cockpit with molded-in dash-to-floor and overhead consoles. ☐ engineered to accept all VW chassis, including the Variant fastback/squareback. This means you can construct your Amante with front discs and fuel-injected engine. ☐ twelve different exterior styling options at no extra cost

Also available is the Amante Completed Body Assembly including instruments, lights, wiring, etc.—ready to bolt on your chassis and drive away.

If you're wondering about performance—don't. The Amante GT can handle Porsche, Corvair and small V-8 engines. Even tube-frame chassis and mid-ship mills.

The Amante GT —a unique American sports car assembly hand-crafted in the European tradition. And it can be yours so easily . . . to build, to own, to drive with pride.

For complete details, specifications, prices and a full-color brochure of The Amante GT, send $2.00 to: Voegele Industries, Dept. CD, 858 Aldo Avenue, Santa Clara, California 95052

Voegele Industries, Dept. CD, 858 Aldo Avenue, Santa Clara, California 95052
Yes! Enclosed is $2.00. Rush me complete details, specifications, prices and a full-color brochure of The Amante GT.

[name—please print]   [address]

[city]   [state]   [zip]

Mercury Capri. For all the hardships the 914, always a Porsche in North America, was a good driving sports car that sold okay. The layout of front MacPherson struts and rear semi-trailing arm suspension followed the VW Type 4, so too the presence of four coils. The 914's base engine was also always VW Type 4 sourced. This started with the Bosch D-jet injected 80bhp 1.7-liter flat-four.

The upscale Porsche 914/6, used the Porsche 911T's 2-liter flat-six. However, with a debut price of $6099 it

The Amante GT was yet another fiberglass-bodied sports car kit, based on the Beetle floorpan. It could accept a variety of motors – girl not included! (Courtesy Voegele Industries)

The Fourteener was foiled by a strong Deutschmark, Datsun 240Z and VW making Porsche pay a high price for Karmann's 914 bodies.
Right: The VW-Porsche 914 used the same 1700 engine and suspension layout as VW's 411E. (Courtesy Lars Sellbom)

was expensive, and sales were always glacial. Just 3318 914/6s were sold, before it gave way to the 1973-76 Porsche 914 2.0. This good selling edition was much better value, and utilized a 100 horse 2-liter version of the Type 4 motor. Porsche also built 11 916 prototypes, with their 2.4-liter flat-six, but this iteration never saw series production. Nor did Ferdinand Piëch's 908 powered 914/8.

The 914's appearance, dubbed the Square Porsche, and the presence of the mighty 911, were tough hurdles to straddle. However,

it did have successes. In 1972 the Fourteener was West Germany's No 1 selling sports car. The roadster came 6th outright at 1970's 24 Hours of Le Mans, and did a 1-2-3 at the Marathon de la Route that same year too. The 914 was Porsche designed, and made good on Ferry Porsche's original intention to make the Porsche 356 mid-engined. As with all air-cooled Porsches, the 914 has been appreciating in value over time, especially the 914/6. It took a while, but the Fourteener finally crossed that finish line!

APPENDIX C
VW OFF-ROAD

THE KÜBELWAGEN, COUNTRY BUGGY & THE THING!

Thanks to Dr Porsche's engineering with the Beetle, VW was destined to dominate on and off-road. It all started pretty soon after the first Bug, as Hitler's war plan sped into action. A need for an all-terrain military vehicle saw the Beetle adapted by Porsche for this purpose. The Beetle's flat floorpan, lightweight and good rear-engined traction made it a natural. The solution for low range gearing was solved by reduction hubs, that utilized spur gears. The result of all this was the rebodied Kübelwagen or bucket car.

This 1971 Type 181 was originally delivered to the Austrian army. Modifications include lowered airbag suspension, with 17x7in replica Fuchs. (Courtesy Marco)

Custom body mods have facilitated the use of Austrian license plates, and a lowered front bumper. Indeed, this Type 181 body has been PU coated, swimming pool style, inside and out. (Courtesy Marco)

The reason the Kübelwagen wasn't converted to more widespread usage with all-wheel drive is unclear. However, the 1942 Type 166 amphibious Schwimmwagen was a 4x4. This system was then applied to a few Kübelwagens (Type 128) and Beetles (Type 87). War output saw around 48,500 Kübelwagens made. It did quite well in its role, but had limitations. Unlike the purpose-designed Jeep, the Kübelwagen was an adapted road car (Beetle), and showed durability problems with heavy usage. That said, the addition of Continental 690-200 balloon tires made the Kübelwagen excellent on sandy terrain. Something for a peacetime future.

The Kübelwagen concept lay dormant for many years, until the early '60s when a NATO need for a military off-road vehicle became apparent. With some development work VW came up with the Type 181. The Type 181 was very much a modern incarnation of the Kübelwagen, but with a few concessions to modernity and comfort. However, that Porsche all independent torsion bar front, swing axle rear suspension was still present and useful off-road. The Type 181's corrugated body panels improved the open vehicle's rigidity, as per the Kübelwagen.

The reincarnated Kübelwagen was known for its fold down windshield, removable side screens and very basic nature. It used the biggest Bug motor around at the time, the 1500 at first, then the 1600 twin port for 1971. From August 1969 through 1973 production

Type 181s do have better engine accessibility than a Beetle. This engine compartment has been further cleaned up by placing electrical wiring in the ammunition boxes for that showcar touch. (Courtesy Marco)

Harley Davidson mirrors are a Brooks Stevens/Type 4 connection. Front bench seat, and special dashboard instruments are further custom touches. Inside, a handmade wooden footrest makes things comfier! (Courtesy Marco)

was at Hanover, with all military versions coming from this plant. There was also production from the Mexican Puebla plant. Type 181 manufacture continued until July 1979, when its role was taken by the VW Iltis. VWoA had tested the Type 181 in America in 1970, but it wasn't until 1973 that it was officially available in this market. In the USA it was dubbed 'The Thing.' US bound Things had standard Eberspacher heaters, and one could specify fancy dress-up interior and exterior items. Functional options included a rollbar and electric winch. The former was very advisable from a safety perspective.

Soon, the Thing had a run in with federal regulators. By the end of 1974 it lost its multi-purpose vehicle exemption, which had allowed it to skip most passenger car safety requirements. Some sales of existing stock lingered on into 1975 model year. In the UK the Thing was called the Trekker, with such RHD market versions designated Type 182. Around 300 were imported, and the Eberspacher was optional. Either way the Thing/Trekker was always pricey, being on par with a top spec Super Beetle (1303S). Still, its unique nature and properties in the new car market made it an invaluable one of a kind thing!

Even more basic than the Type 181/182 was the VW Country Buggy from VW Australia. It was the only vehicle designed by that overseas subsidiary. The Country Buggy's body allowed more ground clearance, and approach/departure angles

commensurate with more serious off-roading. Stock motor was a 1200, with a 1300 and heater both optional. It was a two-seater with rear load area, and a weatherproof tent-like top added some civility. The American market Thing even offered a/c as a dealer installed option. However, as with Country Buggy, basic was best. In arid country areas, the lack of a radiator was a boon.

BAJA BUG
A cheaper way, sort of, to utilize the Type 1's natural off-road abilities was to alter the bodywork of a Beetle.

This 1967 Baja Bug has been lifted three inches. A 1967 T2 transaxle complements big nut reduction boxes, and a modified Scat super diff. The rear suspension has 27mm Sway-A-Way torsion bars and spring plates. (Courtesy Jamie Wiseman)

El Burro has 2006 Honda Civic seats, a GPS speedo, tach, cylinder head temperature gauge, and even an AEM Wideband AFR gauge. It packs a Kerosene 12 volt parking heater, a custom a/c system, and dual batteries! (Courtesy Jamie Wiseman)

Bottom left: For excellent ground covering, 30x9.50-15 mud tires are fitted to 15x7in rims. A 1⅜in Sidewinder exhaust and repositioned muffler aid exhalation. (Courtesy Jamie Wiseman)

The result would be the iconic Baja Bug. The moniker came from the geographical location. And of course, said Bug made a name for itself, from success in the famous Mexican 1000 off-road race. It's believed the first Baja Bug was built by Gary Emory in 1968, courtesy of his company Parts Obsolete. The first race with a Baja Bug was naturally the 1968 Mexican 1000. Driving that Baja Bug was legendary artist and designer Dave 'Big' Deal. He was an exponent of air-cooled VWs in more ways than one The final historical first was the first 'Bug Eye' Baja Bug kit, from Miller-Havens in 1969.

There was never a factory Baja Bug from VW. No, one had to create a Baja Bug, using an aftermarket kit, or a personal custom job. Two main avenues were the 'Wide Eye' method, where the headlamps remained in the usual VW Beetle fender location. The aforementioned Bug Eye kit saw the headlamps relocated to an inner fiberglass nosepiece, associated with smaller custom fenders. Headlamps are heavy, and to stop them moving about due to the Baja Bug's flexible fiberglass fenders, the Bug Eye kit has its advantages. A typical Baja Bug conversion runs to a truncated

This is a Sand Scorcher Baja Bug kit, from Tamiya. This rear-engined ¹⁄₁₀ scale electric RC kit has pre Super Beetle VW suspension. That is, torsion bars at the front and a rear swing axle. (Author)

fiberglass hood/nose section, four fiberglass fenders, and an abbreviated engine lid. Said lid has a raised center section, for an oversize air cleaner. Fitting all of the above necessitates cutting stock Beetle bodywork, like inner fenders.

With a Baja Bug bigger wheels can be fitted. Indeed, removing suspension stops facilitates suspension travel. It all depends how serious the purpose at hand is. In the case of ex jet pilot Michael E Long, very serious. When writing an article for *National Geographic* on Baja California, he teamed up with the journal's ad man Dick Lehman, to do the 1972 Mexican 1000. Long called his Baja Bug 'Boojum' after the Baja region's famous tree.

In spite of an HD clutch, shocks, rollbar, oversize tires and skidplate, Boojum suffered four broken shocks and three failed axle bearings. The Bug Eyed Boojum finally expired, due to a broken axle bearing after 565 miles of the race's 832 miles. It finally broke down at Los Dolores, which means The Sorrows.[25] To show how tough air-cooled VWs are, and the Mexican

1980 F1 champion Alan Jones inspects Tamiya Sand Scorchers, decorated in Williams Team livery. (Courtesy Tamiya Plastic Model Co)

1000 for that matter, another Baja Bug utilized condensed milk through the tire's valve to seal a punctured inner tube. The fix lasted 430 miles … then the clutch broke!

DUNE BUGGY & SAND RAIL

If you have the world's most popular car at hand, there are going to be plenty of base cars to build an off-roader from. The VW dune buggy was a natural for the car-customizing

This 1969 Beetle has been converted to a Bug Eye Baja Bug, using a Mark V Fiberglass kit. However, the original Beetle steel hood and engine lid have been retained and reshaped. The original Type 1 1500 has been replaced by a 2002 Chevy Cavalier ECOTEC 2.2-liter I4. The radiator is in front of the motor. This Baja Bug utilizes electric power steering.

The color is Kubota Orange, with a flattening agent for a satin finish. 15in Federal Couragia MT tires, four-wheel disk brakes, and Porsche 944 outer stub axles are employed. Type 181 spindles and trailing arms helped lift the front end by 3in.
Delicacy of the MacPherson strut front suspension made the non Super Beetle the Bug of choice for off-road Baja conversions. (All four photographs courtesy Lagler Automotive Specialties)

scene of the '60s and '70s. It was more elaborate than cutting Beetle bodywork, but did utilize Bug underpinnings. Just unbolt the Beetle body from the T1 floorpan, add a trick fiberglass body and voila! An instant dune buggy was created. Once again, you couldn't get a factory job from VW. Just go aftermarket and do it yourself.

Dune buggies were typically based on the Type 1 Beetle platform. Bruce Meyers' Meyers Manx was the first kit-based buggy. A Meyers Manx, like this buggy, was featured in the Elvis Presley 1968 movie Live A Little, Love A Little. Due to extra cost and weight, the Type 4 motors didn't figure greatly in dune buggy usage. (Author)

The first fellow credited with coming up with the dune buggy concept was Bruce Meyers with his 1964 Meyers Manx. Meyers patented the Manx, but that didn't stop market newcomers driving to the dunes. As expected it was a fiberglass mold bolted to Type 1 platform, with some truncation of the rear part of the Beetle's chassis. The latter action implied shorter pipework and cables. The dune buggy was the new T-bucket! Volksrod rolled in, arriving in the UK via a Doncaster importer, in the first week of September 1967. Just one week later, it was the turn of the GP Buggy.

GP Beach Buggies UK was in Brentford, and was founded by South African race mechanic Paul du Plessis. In America the dune buggy market was running at 5000 units per year. Worldwide the phenomenon peaked during the late '60s to the early '70s as a sports car, convertible alternative. At the cinema a yellow Meyers Manx was driven by Elvis Presley's photographer character Greg Nolan, in the 1968 movie *Live A Little, Love A Little*. The VW dune buggy also starred in *The Thomas Crown Affair*, followed by Paul Newman's racing film *Winning* in 1969. In 1974, a red Italian Puma dune buggy was featured in the Bud Spencer/Terence Hill movie, *Watch Out, We're Mad!*

Due to weight and cost, the Type 4 411/412 motor wasn't much fitted to the dune buggy species. However, off-road racing specialization doesn't come cheap, and VW off-road racing doesn't get much more custom, than a VW sand rail. This involves a purpose-built tubular chassis frame, and lightweight VW air-cooled motor. Chenowth is a well known sand rail chassis maker, and any engine can be mounted, not just VW units.

Top: This Al Smith (Smith Sandcars) design sand rail has a traditional swing axle, 4.86:1 final drive, close ratio Weddle gears from 2nd to 4th, and a Berg shifter.

Center: A 2332 flat-four with dual 44s and 1.5in dual Cannon exhaust system powers this VW sand rail. A super-diff and Autolinea case are further upgrades.

Bottom: As was discovered from Kübelwagens in WWII, the combination of VW's lightweight, rear-engined traction and balloon tires made for formidable off-road ability. (Courtesy Mike)

You want traction? You got traction! Rear-engined VWs were useful in slippery conditions. (Courtesy Mot)

APPENDIX D

VOLKSWAGEN GROUP AREAS OF INTEREST

www.type4.org
Started by Jens Vagelpohl in 1999, Type 4.org is an informational resource website, on the largest air-cooled car VW ever made.

www.vwtype3and4club.org.uk
The VW Type 3 & 4 Club (UK) caters to owners in Great Britain, but also has a forum for owners and fans of the low profile flat-four powered Vee Dubs.

www.vwloosenuts.com
Vancouver, Washington based air-cooled VW specialist Loose Nuts does unique things to Dr Porsche's early work, such as Safari window kits for Type 1 and Type 3 Squareback.

www.thesamba.com
For all your air-cooled needs, with forums that include Type 4 and Porsches.

www.fvwa.fi
If Finland is your neck of the woods, then the Finnish Volkswagen Association FVWA is your club!

The evergreen Beetle in Colombo, Sri Lanka. (Courtesy Bandula Kodituwakku)

www.gilmore-enterprises.net
Ed Muha founded Gilmore Enterprises, the go-to place to get air-conditioning into an air-cooled VW, or indeed get your classic VW A/C functioning again. They do VW Type 4, Porsche 914 and 912s too.

www.audicentreperth.com.au
The Audi Centre Perth is your first stop, for Ingolstadt's finest in Perth, Western Australia – the state's only authorized Audi dealer!

Miru the cat with a chocolate Bug! (Courtesy http://www016.upp.so-net.ne.jp/MARIERIKA/)

BIBLIOGRAPHY

Autotest, "Volkswagen 411L two door No.2214." *Autocar*, November 14 1968.

Consumer Reports, 1970, p439.

Consumer Reports. "Two New Small Cars." *Consumer Reports*, July 1975.

Davis, Pedr. "The Wankel – In The Home Stretch?" *Wheels*, February 1968.

Grove, Noel. "Swing Low, Sweet Chariot!" *National Geographic*, July 1983.

Hibbard, Jeff. *Baja Bugs & Buggies*. New York: HP Books Inc, 1983.

Holmes, Mark. *Ultimate Convertibles – Roofless Beauty*. London: Kandour Ltd, 2007.

Holusha, John. "Volkswagen to Shut US Plant." *New York Times*, 21 November 1987.

Joslin, Bryan. "1951-62 Mercedes-Benz 300: Return to Greatness." *Collectible Automobile*, June 2015.

Kenwright, Joe. "Hatchback Genesis Golf versus Astina." *Australian VW Power*, June/July 1992.

Long, Michael E. "Driving The Mexican 1000 Rocks, Ruts and Sand." *National Geographic*, October 1972.

Ludvigsen, Karl. "Fuel Injection: One Answer To Smog?" *Motor Trend*, March 1968.

MacCana, Aongus. "Gathering of the clan." *VW Motoring*, September 1992.

Madow, Marc. "As Japanese As Pizza." *CAR*, October 1972.

Meredith, Laurence. "Man of the People's Car." *Thoroughbred & Classic Cars*, September 1994.

Nicholas, Nick. "Russell's Type 181." *Australian VW Power*, June/July 1992.

Nichols, Mel. "Schizophrenic Mazda RX-2." *Wheels*, January 1971.

Putman, John J. "Continuing Miracle." *National Geographic*, August 1977.

Road & Track. "R&T Specifications 1975." *Road & Track*, February 1975.

Robson, Graham. *Classic & Sportscar A-Z Of Cars of the 1970s*. Devon: Bay View Books Ltd, 1990.

Seidler, Edouard. "Miracle Man." *Autocar*, 31 July 1985.

Wager, Paul. *Beetle Mania*. London: Bison Books Ltd, 1995.

Walton, Paul. "Birth Right." Thoroughbred & Classic Cars, December 1999.

Young, Ian. "Brazilian Affair." *Thoroughbred & Classic Cars*, June 1993.

FOOTNOTES

[*] Autotest, "Volkswagen 411L two door No.2214." *Autocar* (November 14 1968): p12

[1] Laurence Meredith, "Man of the People's Car." *Thoroughbred & Classic Cars* (September 1994): p73

[2] Paul Wager, Beetle Mania. (London: Bison Books Ltd, 1995): p14

[3] Ibid. p52

[4] *Consumer Reports* 1970 p439.

[5] Bryan Joslin, "1951-62 Mercedes-Benz 300: Return to Greatness." *Collectible Automobile* (June 2015): p76

[6] Mel Nichols, "Schizophrenic Mazda RX-2." *Wheels* (January 1971): p15

[7] Nick Nicholas, "Russell's Type 181." *Australian VW Power* (June/July 1992): p59

[8] Karl Ludvigsen, "Fuel Injection: One Answer To Smog?" *Motor Trend* (March 1968): p40

[9] Pedr Davis, "The Wankel – In The Home Stretch?" *Wheels* (February 1968): p41

[10] Marc Madow, "As Japanese As Pizza." *CAR* (October 1972): p40

[11] Graham Robson, *Classic & Sportscar A-Z Of Cars of the 1970s*. (Devon: Bay View Books Ltd, 1990): p176

[12] Aongus MacCana, "Gathering of the clan." *VW Motoring* (September 1992): p31

[13] Wager, op cit. p54

[14] Jeff Hibbard, *Baja Bugs & Buggies*. (New York: HP Books Inc, 1983): p44

[15] *Road & Track*, "R&T Specifications 1975." *Road & Track* (February 1975): p94

[16] John J. Putman, "Continuing Miracle." *National Geographic* (August 1977): p161

[17] Edouard Seidler, "Miracle Man." *Autocar* (31 July 1985): p39

[18] *Consumer Reports*, "Two New Small Cars." *Consumer Reports* (July 1975): p408

[19] Paul Walton, "Birth Right." *Thoroughbred & Classic Cars* (December 1999): p 88

[20] John Holusha, "Volkswagen to Shut U.S. Plant." *New York Times* (21 November 1987): p1

[21] Noel Grove, "Swing Low, Sweet Chariot!" *National Geographic* (July 1983): p13

[22] Joe Kenwright, "Hatchback Genesis Golf versus Astina." *Australian VW Power* (June/July 1992): p8

[23] Mark Holmes, *Ultimate Convertibles – Roofless Beauty*. (London: Kandour Ltd, 2007): p157

[24] Ian Young, "Brazilian Affair." *Thoroughbred & Classic Cars* (June 1993): p57

[25] Michael E. Long, "Driving The Mexican 1000 Rocks, Ruts and Sand." *National Geographic* (October 1972): p575

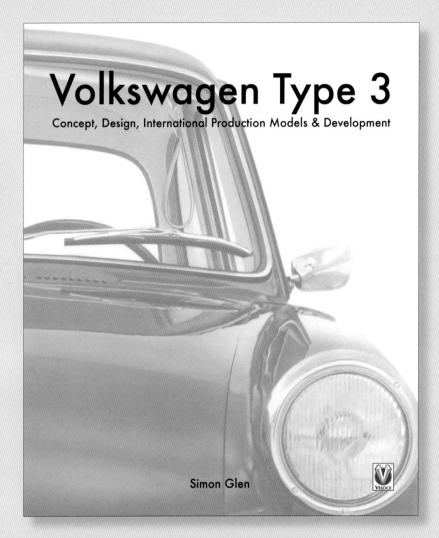

Volkswagen Type 3

Concept, Design, International Production Models & Development

Simon Glen

The definitive international story of the Volkswagen Type 3. Simon Glen writes from first-hand experience, having owned seven Type 3s – five Variants, a 1500 Notchback and a 1500S Karmann·Ghia – which have been driven through Africa, Europe, Australia and New Zealand.

ISBN: 978-1-845849-52-8
Hardback • 25x20.7cm • 160 pages • 1114 pictures

For more information and price details, visit our website at www.veloce.co.uk • email: info@veloce.co.uk
• Tel: +44(0)1305 260068

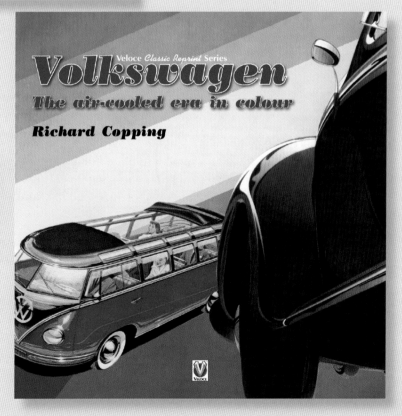

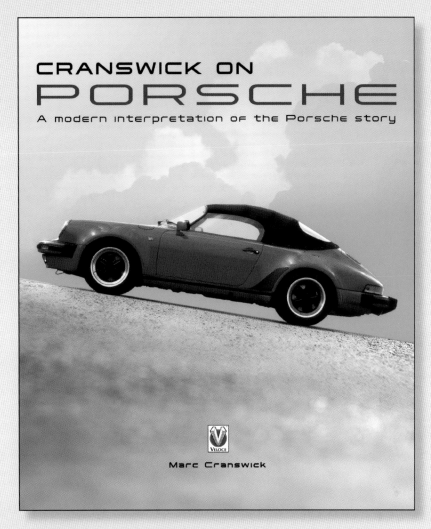

INDEX